TAO OF JEET KUNE DO

by

This Book is Dedicated to the Free, Creative
Martial Artist
Take what is useful and develop from there.

ACKNOWLEDGEMENTS

Grateful acknowledgement is made to the copyright owners for permission to reprint or adapt from the following: *Boxing*, by Edwin L. Haislet, 1940, The Ronald Press, pp. 33-34, 47, 72, 97-99, 106, 128, 149-150, 154-155, 158-159, 173, 178-180. *Fencing*, by Hugo and James Castello, 1962, The Ronald Press, pp. 139-140, 144. *Fencing with the Foil*, by Roger Crosnier, 1951, A.S. Barnes and Co., pp. 132-135, 137-139, 168, 170-171, 182-184. *The Theory and Practice of Fencing*, by Julio Martinez Castello, 1933, Charles Scribner's Sons, pp. 43, 44, 62, 63, 125, 127, 133-136, 139, 145, 168, 191.

WARNING

OHARA PUBLICATIONS, INCORPORATED. 24715 Avenue Rockefeller, P.O. Box 918, Santa Clarita, California 91380-9018

武道釋義

Into a soul absolutely free
From thoughts and emotion,
Even the tiger finds no room
To insert its fierce claws.

One and the same breeze passes
Over the pines on the mountain
And the oak trees in the valley;
And why do they give different notes?

No thinking, no reflecting,
Perfect emptiness;
Yet therein something moves,
Following its own course.

The eye sees it,
But no hands can take hold of it —
The moon in the stream.

Clouds and mists,
They are midair transformations;
Above them eternally shine the sun and the moon.

Victory is for the one,
Even before the combat,
Who has no thought of himself,
Abiding in the no-mind-ness of Great Origin.

A Taoist Priest

THE MARTIAL ARTS INCLUDING BOXING

The martial arts are based upon understanding, hard work and a total comprehension of skills. Power training and the use of force are easy, but total comprehension of all of the skills of the martial arts is very difficult to achieve. To understand you must study all of natural movement in all living things. Naturally, you can understand the martial arts of others. You can study the timing and the weaknesses. Just knowing these two elements will give you the capacity to knock him down rather easily.

THE HEART OF THE MARTIAL ARTS IS IN UNDERSTANDING TECHNIQUES

To understand techniques you must learn that they contain a lot of condensed movement. This may look quite awkward. When you start to learn it you will find that it is awkward to you. That is because a good technique includes quick changes, great variety and speed. It may be a system of reversals much like a concept of God and the Devil. In the speed of events, which one is really in charge? Do they change places with lightning speed? The Chinese believe so. To put the heart of the martial arts in your own heart and have it be a part of you means total comprehension and the use of a free style. When you have that you will know that there are no limits.

「拳道」與拳術

　拳道以意會　力拙尚意巧　力易尚意難.
若要內自然動靜中悟出萬物變化之
理自萬物變化之理中悟出別人之拳
法之節奏破綻乘虛而入.如水滲隙

「心拳」與術拳

　大巧若拙　拙中之巧　返璞歸真
內蘊天地變化之機　外藏鬼神
莫測之變

「哲藝」之境

　有些武術雖然先聲奪人　但卻如喝滲
水之酒　令人越飲越覺無味　但有些武
術其味雖覺苦澀　但卻如細嚼橄欖
便令人越想越是回味無窮.

「入世」與「出世」

　不再以出世為修練拳道的途徑而完
全入世了　如佛門弟子心經入世
的修為方為正果.
此書入世之後便可自紅塵中修
學以前無從學到的自然平常的
路徑.

PRECAUTIONS ON PHYSICAL TECHNIQUES

Some martial arts are very popular, real crowd pleasers, because they look good, have smooth techniques. But beware. They are like a wine that has been watered. A diluted wine is not a real wine, not a good wine, hardly the genuine article.

Some martial arts don't look so good, but you know that they have a kick, a tang, a genuine taste. They are like olives. The taste may be strong and bitter-sweet. The flavor lasts. You cultivate a taste for them. No one ever developed a taste for diluted wine.

ACQUIRED TALENT AND NATURAL TALENT

Some people are born with good physiques, a sense of speed and a lot of stamina. That's fine. But in the martial arts everything you learn is an acquired skill.

Absorbing a martial art is like the experience of Buddhism. The feeling for it comes from the heart. You have the dedication to get what you know you need. When it becomes part of you, you know you have it. You succeed at it. You may never fully understand all of it, but you keep at it. And as you progress you know the true nature of the simple way. You may join a temple or a kwoon. You observe nature's simple way. You experience a life you never had before.

Translation: David Koong Pak Sen

INTRODUCTION

My husband Bruce always considered himself a martial artist first and an actor second. At the age of 13, Bruce started lessons in the wing chun style of gung-fu for the purpose of self-defense. Over the next 19 years, he transformed his knowledge into a science, an art, a philosophy and a way of life. He trained his body through exercise and practice; he trained his mind through reading and reflecting and he recorded his thoughts and ideas constantly over the 19 years. The pages of this book represent the pride of a life's work.

In his lifelong quest for self-knowledge and personal expression, Bruce was constantly studying, analyzing and modifying all available relative information; his principle source was his personal library which consisted of over 2,000 books dealing with all forms of physical conditioning, martial arts, fighting techniques, defenses and related subjects.

In 1970, Bruce sustained a rather severe injury to his back. His doctors ordered him to discontinue the practice of martial arts and to remain in bed to allow his back to heal. This was probably the most trying and dispiriting time in Bruce's life. He stayed in bed, virtually flat on his back for six months, but he couldn't keep his mind from working — the result of which is this book. The bulk of these writings was done at that time, but many scattered notes were recorded at earlier and later times. Bruce's personal study notes reveal that he was particularly impressed by the writings of Edwin L. Haislet, Julio Martinez Castello, Hugo and James Castello and Roger Crosnier. Many of Bruce's own theories are directly related to those expressed by these writers.

Bruce had decided to finish the book in 1971 but his film work kept him from completing it. He also vacillated about the advisability of publishing his work because he felt it might be used for wrong purposes. He did not intend it to be a "how-to" book or a "learn kung-fu in 10 easy lessons" book. He intended it as a record of one man's way of thinking and as a guide, not a set of instructions. If you can read it in this light, there is much to be aware of on these pages. And, you probably will have many questions, the answers to which you must seek within yourself. When you have finished this book, you will know Bruce Lee better, but hopefully you will also know yourself better.

Now, open your mind and read, understand, and experience, and when you've reached that point, discard this book. The pages are best used for cleaning up a mess — as you will see.

Linda Lee

In the hands of a singular man, simple things carefully placed ring with an undeniable harmony. Bruce's orchestration of martial arts had that quality, most apparent in his combat motion. Immobilized for several months with an injured back, he picked up a pen. There, too, he wrote as he spoke, as he moved — with directness and with honesty.

Like listening to a musical composition, understanding the elements within it adds a specialness to the sound. For this reason, Linda Lee and I are liberalizing the introduction of Bruce's book to explain how it came about.

The *Tao of Jeet Kune Do* actually began before Bruce was born. The classical wing chun style that started him on his way was developed 400 years before his time. The 2,000 or so books he owned and the countless books he read, described the individual "discoveries" of thousands of men before him. There's nothing new within this book; there are no secrets. "It's nothing special," Bruce used to say. And so it wasn't.

Bruce's special key was knowing himself and his own capabilities to correctly choose things that worked for him and to convey those things in movement and in language. He found in the philosophies of Confucius, Spinoza, Krishnamurti and others, an organization for his concepts and, with that organization, he began the book of his tao.

The book when he died was only partially completed. Though it spanned seven volumes, it filled only one. Between major blocks of copy were unnumbered pages of unused paper, each headed by simple titles. Sometimes he wrote introspectively, asking questions of himself. More often he wrote to his invisible student, the reader. When he wrote quickly, he sacrificed his practiced grammar and when he took his time, he was eloquent.

Some of the material within the volumes was written in a single setting and had the natural progression of a well-outlined conversation. Other areas were sudden inspirations and incomplete ideas that were quickly scribbled as they entered Bruce's head. These were scattered throughout the work. In addition to the seven hardbound volumes, Bruce wrote notes throughout the development of his Jeet Kune Do and left them in stacks and drawers among his belongings. Some were outdated and others were more recent and still valuable to his book.

With the help of his wife, Linda, I collected and scanned and thoroughly indexed all the material. Then, I tried to draw the scattered ideas together into cohesive blocks. Most of the copy was left unchanged and the drawings and sketches are his own.

The book's organization, however, could not have been justly done were it not for the patient attention of Danny Inosanto, his assistant instructors and class of senior students. It was they who took my eight years of martial arts training, threw it out on the floor and turned the theories into action with *their* knowledge. They have my gratitude both as the editor of this book and, separately, as a martial artist.

It should be mentioned that the *Tao of Jeet Kune Do* is not complete. Bruce's art was changing every day. Within the Five Ways of Attack, for instance, he originally began with a category called *hand immobilization.* Later, he found that too limiting since immobilizations could be applied to the legs and arms and head as well. It was a simple observation that showed the limits of attaching labels to any concept.

The *Tao of Jeet Kune Do* has no real ending. It serves, instead, as a beginning. It has no style; it has no level, though it's most easily read by those who understand their weapons. To probably every statement within the book, there is an exception — no book could give a total picture of the combat arts. This is simply a work that describes the direction of Bruce's studies. The investigations are left undone; the questions, some elementary and some complex, are left unanswered to make the student question for himself. Likewise, the drawings are often unexplained and may offer only vague impressions. But if they spark a question, if they raise an idea, they serve a purpose.

Hopefully, this book will be used as a source of ideas for all martial artists, ideas that should then develop further. Inevitably and regrettably, the book may also cause a rash of "Jeet Kune Do" schools, headed by people who know the reputation of the name and very little about the movement. Beware of such schools! If their instructors missed the last, most important line, chances are they failed to understand the book at all.

Even the organization of the book means nothing. There are no real lines between speed and power, or between precision and kicking, or hand strikes and range; each element of combat movement affects those around it. The divisions I've made are only for convenient reading — don't take them too seriously. Use a pencil as you read and cross reference the related areas you find. Jeet Kune Do, you see, has no definite lines or boundaries — only those you make yourself.

Gilbert L. Johnson

武
道
釋
義

CONTENTS

ON ZEN

To obtain enlightenment in martial art means the extinction of everything which obscures the "true knowledge," the "real life." At the same time, it implies *boundless expansion* and, indeed, emphasis should fall not on the cultivation of the particular department which merges into the totality, but rather on the totality that enters and unites that particular department.

―――――――――――――――

The way to transcend *karma* lies in the proper use of the mind and the will. The oneness of all life is a truth that can be fully realized only when false notions of a separate self, whose destiny can be considered apart from the whole, are forever annihilated.

―――――――――――――――

Voidness is that which stands right in the middle between this and that. The void is all-inclusive, having no opposite — there is nothing which it excludes or opposes. It is living void, because all forms come out of it and whoever realizes the void is filled with life and power and the love of all beings.

―――――――――――――――

Turn into a doll made of wood: it has no ego, it thinks nothing, it is not grasping or sticky. Let the body and limbs work themselves out in accordance with the discipline they have undergone.

The consciousness of self is the greatest hindrance to the proper execution of all physical action.

―――――――――――――――

If nothing within you stays rigid, outward things will disclose themselves. Moving, be like water. Still, be like a mirror. Respond like an echo.

―――――――――――――――

Nothingness cannot be defined; the softest thing cannot be snapped.

―――――――――――――――

I'm moving and not moving at all. I'm like the moon underneath the waves that ever go on rolling and rocking. It is not, "I am doing this," but rather, an inner realization that "this is happening through me," or "it is doing this for me." The consciousness of self is the greatest hindrance to the proper execution of all physical action.

―――――――――――――――

The localization of the mind means its freezing. When it ceases to flow freely as it is needed, it is no more the mind in its suchness.

The "Immovable" is the concentration of energy at a given focus, as at the axis of a wheel, instead of dispersal in scattered activities.

———————————————

The point is the doing of them rather than the accomplishments. There is no actor but the action; there is no experiencer but the experience.

———————————————

To see a thing uncolored by one's own personal preferences and desires is to see it in its own pristine simplicity.

———————————————

Art reaches its greatest peak when devoid of self-consciousness. Freedom discovers man the moment he loses concern over what impression he is making or about to make.

———————————————

To see a thing uncolored by one's own personal preferences and desires is to see it in its own pristine simplicity.

The perfect way is only difficult for those who pick and choose. Do not like, do not dislike; all will then be clear. Make a hairbreadth difference and heaven and earth are set apart; if you want the truth to stand clear before you, never be for or against. The struggle between "for" and "against" is the mind's worst disease.

———————————————

Wisdom does not consist of trying to wrest the good from the evil but in learning to "ride" them as a cork adapts itself to the crests and troughs of the waves.

———————————————

Let yourself go with the disease, be with it, keep company with it — this is the way to be rid of it.

———————————————

An assertion is Zen only when it is itself an act and does not refer to anything that is asserted in it.

———————————————

In Buddhism, there is no place for using effort. Just be ordinary and nothing special. Eat your food, move your bowels, pass water and when you're tired go and lie down. The ignorant will laugh at me, but the wise will understand.

———————————————

Establish nothing in regard to oneself. Pass quickly like the non-existent and be quiet as purity. Those who gain lose. Do not precede others, always follow them.

Do not run away; let go. Do not seek, for it will come when least expected.

———————— ·•· ————————

Give up thinking as though not giving it up. Observe techniques as though not observing.

———————— ·•· ————————

There is no fixed teaching. All I can provide is an appropriate medicine for a particular ailment.

———————— ·•· ————————

Buddhism's Eight-Fold Path

The eight requirements to eliminate suffering by correcting false values and giving true knowledge of life's meaning have been summed up as follows:

1. *Right views (understanding):* You must see clearly what is wrong.
2. *Right purpose (aspiration):* Decide to be cured.
3. *Right speech:* Speak so as to aim at being cured.
4. *Right conduct:* You must act.
5. *Right vocation:* Your livelihood must not conflict with your therapy.
6. *Right effort:* The therapy must go forward at the "staying speed," the critical velocity that can be sustained.
7. *Right awareness (mind control):* You must feel it and think about it incessantly.
8. *Right concentration (meditation):* Learn how to contemplate with the deep mind.

There is no fixed teaching. All I can provide is an appropriate medicine for a particular ailment.

———————— ·•· ————————

ART OF THE SOUL

The aim of art is to project an inner vision into the world, to state in aesthetic creation the deepest psychic and personal experiences of a human being. It is to enable those experiences to be intelligible and generally recognized within the total framework of an ideal world.

———————— ·•· ————————

Art reveals itself in psychic understanding of the inner essence of things and gives form to the relation of man with *nothing*, with the nature of the absolute.

———————— ·•· ————————

Art is an expression of life and transcends both time and space. We must employ our

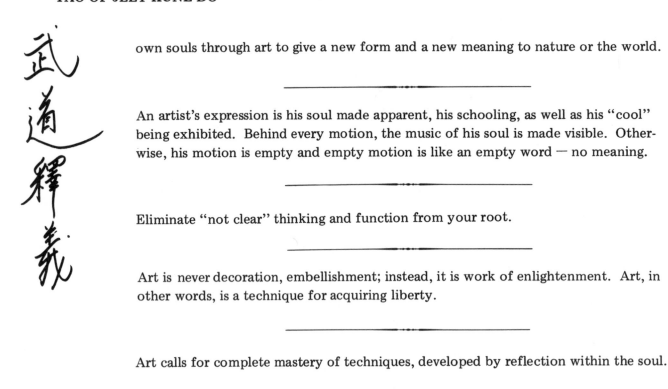

own souls through art to give a new form and a new meaning to nature or the world.

———————————

An artist's expression is his soul made apparent, his schooling, as well as his "cool" being exhibited. Behind every motion, the music of his soul is made visible. Otherwise, his motion is empty and empty motion is like an empty word — no meaning.

———————————

Eliminate "not clear" thinking and function from your root.

———————————

Art is never decoration, embellishment; instead, it is work of enlightenment. Art, in other words, is a technique for acquiring liberty.

———————————

Art calls for complete mastery of techniques, developed by reflection within the soul.

———————————

"Artless art" is the artistic process within the artist; its meaning is *art of the soul.*

"Artless art" is the artistic process within the artist; its meaning is *"art of the soul."*
All the various moves of all the tools means a step on the way to the absolute aesthetic world of the soul.

———————————

Creation in art is the psychic unfolding of the personality, which is rooted in the *nothing.* Its effect is a deepening of the personal dimension of the soul.

———————————

The artless art is the art of the soul at peace, like moonlight mirrored in a deep lake. The ultimate aim of the artist is to use his daily activity to become a past master of life, and so lay hold of the art of living. Masters in all branches of art must first be masters of living, for the soul creates everything.

———————————

All vague notions must fall before a pupil can call himself a master.

———————————

Art is the way to the *absolute* and to the essence of human life. The aim of art is not the one-sided promotion of spirit, soul and senses, but the *opening* of all human capacities — thought, feeling, will — to the life rhythm of the world of nature. So will the voiceless voice be heard and the self be brought into harmony with it.

Artistic skill, therefore, does not mean artistic perfection. It remains rather a continuing medium or reflection of some step in psychic development, the perfection of which is not to be found in shape and form, but must radiate from the human soul.

The artistic activity does not lie in art itself as such. It penetrates into a deeper world in which all art forms (of things inwardly experienced) flow together, and in which the harmony of soul and cosmos in the *nothing* has its outcome in reality.

It is the artistic process, therefore, that is reality and reality is truth.

The Path To Truth
1. SEEKING AFTER TRUTH
2. AWARENESS OF TRUTH (and its existence)
3. PERCEPTION OF TRUTH (its substance and direction — like the perception of movement)
4. UNDERSTANDING OF TRUTH (A first-rate philosopher practices it to understand it — TAO. Not to be fragmented, but to see the totality — Krishnamurti)
5. EXPERIENCING OF TRUTH
6. MASTERING OF TRUTH
7. FORGETTING TRUTH
8. FORGETTING THE CARRIER OF TRUTH
9. RETURN TO THE PRIMAL SOURCE WHERE TRUTH HAS ITS ROOTS
10. *REPOSE IN THE NOTHING*

JEET KUNE DO

It is indeed difficult to see the situation simply — our minds are very complex — and it is easy to teach one to be skillful, but it is difficult to teach one his own attitude.

For security, the unlimited living is turned into something dead, a chosen pattern that limits. To understand Jeet Kune Do, one ought to throw away all ideals, patterns, styles; in fact, he should throw away even the concepts of what is or isn't ideal in Jeet Kune Do. Can you look at a situation without naming it? Naming it, making it a word, causes fear.

It is indeed difficult to see the situation simply — our minds are very complex — and it is easy to teach one to be skillful, but it is difficult to teach him his own attitude.

Jeet Kune Do favors formlessness so that it can assume all forms and since Jeet Kune Do has no style, it can fit in with all styles. As a result, Jeet Kune Do utilizes all ways and is bound by none and, likewise, uses any techniques or means which serve its end.

———

Approach Jeet Kune Do with the idea of mastering the will. Forget about winning and losing; forget about pride and pain. Let your opponent graze your skin and you smash into his flesh; let him smash into your flesh and you fracture his bones; let him fracture your bones and you take his life! Do not be concerned with your escaping safely — lay your life before him!

———

The great mistake is to anticipate the outcome of the engagement; you ought not to be thinking of whether it ends in victory or in defeat. Let nature take its course, and your tools will strike at the right moment.

———

Jeet Kune Do teaches us not to look backward once the course is decided upon. It treats life and death indifferently.

———

Jeet Kune Do avoids the superficial, penetrates the complex, goes to the heart of the problem and pinpoints the key factors.

Jeet Kune Do avoids the superficial, penetrates the complex, goes to the heart of the problem and pinpoints the key factors.

———

Jeet Kune Do does not beat around the bush. It does not take winding detours. It follows a straight line to the objective. *Simplicity is the shortest distance between two points.*

———

The art of Jeet Kune Do is simply to simplify. It is being oneself; it is reality in its "isness." Thus, isness is the meaning — having freedom in its primary sense, not limited by attachments, confinements, partialization, complexities.

———

Jeet Kune Do is the enlightenment. It is a way of life, a movement toward will power and control, though it ought to be enlightened by intuition.

———

While being trained, the student is to be active and dynamic in every way. But in actual combat, his mind must be calm and not at all disturbed. He must feel as if nothing critical is happening. When he advances, his steps should be light and secure, his eyes not fixed and glaring insanely at the enemy. His behavior should not be in any way different from his everyday behavior, no change taking place in his expression, nothing betraying the fact that he is engaged in mortal combat.

The tools, your natural weapons, have a double purpose:

1.   To destroy the opponent in front of you — annihilation of things that stand in the way of peace, justice and humanity.

2.   To destroy your own impulses caused by the instincts of self-preservation. To destroy anything bothering your mind. Not to hurt anyone, but to overcome your own greed, anger and folly. Jeet Kune Do is directed toward oneself.

Punches and kicks are tools to kill the ego. The tools represent the force of intuitive or instinctive directness which, unlike the intellect or the complicated ego, does not divide itself, blocking its own freedom. The tools move onward without looking back or to the side.

Because of the pure-heartedness and empty-mindedness inherent in man, his tools partake of these qualities and play their role with the utmost degree of freedom. The tools stand as symbols of the invisible spirit, keeping the mind, body and limbs in full activity.

The art of Jeet Kune Do is simply to simplify.

Absence of stereotyped technique as the substance means to be total and free. All lines and movements are the function.

Non-attachment as the foundation is man's original nature. In its ordinary process, thought moves forward without halting; past, present and future thoughts continue as an unbroken stream.

Absence of thought as the doctrine means not to be carried away by thought in the process of thought, not to be defiled by external objects, to be in thought yet devoid of thought.

True thusness is the substance of thought and thought is the function of true thusness. To think of thusness, to define it in thought is to defile it.

Bring the mind into sharp focus and make it alert so that it can immediately intuit truth, which is everywhere. The mind must be emancipated from old habits, prejudices, restrictive thought processes and even ordinary thought itself.

Scratch away all the dirt your being has accumulated and reveal reality in its isness, or in its suchness, or in its nakedness, which corresponds to the Buddhist concept of emptiness.

Empty your cup so that it may be filled; become devoid to gain totality.

Empty your cup so that it may be filled; become devoid to gain totality.

ORGANIZED DESPAIR

In the long history of martial arts, the instinct to follow and imitate seems to be inherent in most martial artists, instructors and students alike. This is partly due to human tendency and partly because of the steep traditions behind multiple patterns of styles. Consequently, to find a refreshing, original, master teacher is a rarity. The need for a "pointer of the way" echoes.

Each man belongs to a style which claims to possess truth to the exclusion of all other styles. These styles become institutes with their explanations of the "Way," dissecting and isolating the harmony of firmness and gentleness, establishing rhythmic forms as the particular state of their techniques.

Instead of facing combat in its suchness, then, most systems of martial art accumulate a "fancy mess" that distorts and cramps their practitioners and distracts them from the actual reality of combat, which is simple and direct. Instead of going immediately to the heart of things, flowery forms (organized despair) and artificial techniques are ritualistically practiced to simulate actual combat. Thus, instead of "being" in combat these practitioners are "doing" something "about" combat.

Worse still, super mental power and spiritual this and spiritual that are desperately incorporated until these practitioners drift further and further into mystery and abstraction. All such things are futile attempts to arrest and fix the ever-changing movements in combat and to dissect and analyze them like a corpse.

When you get down to it, real combat is not fixed and is very much "alive." The fancy mess (a form of paralysis) solidifies and conditions what was once fluid, and when you look at it realistically, it is nothing but a blind devotion to the systematic uselessness of practicing routines or stunts that lead nowhere.

———————— ————————

When real feeling occurs, such as anger or fear, can the stylist express himself with the classical method, or is he merely listening to his own screams and yells? Is he a living, expressive human being or merely a patternized mechanical robot? Is he an entity, capable of flowing with external circumstances, or is he resisting with his set of chosen patterns? Is his chosen pattern forming a screen between him and the opponent and preventing a "total" and "fresh" relationship?

———————— ————————

Stylists, instead of looking directly into the fact, cling to forms (theories) and go on entangling themselves further and further, finally putting themselves into an inextricable snare.

———————— ————————

They do not see *it* in its suchness because their indoctrination is crooked and twisted. Discipline must conform to the nature of things in their suchness.

———————— ————————

Maturity does not mean to become a captive of conceptualization. It is the realization of what lies in our innermost selves.

———————— ————————

When there is
freedom from
mechanical con-
ditioning, there
is simplicity.

When there is freedom from mechanical conditioning, there is simplicity. Life is a relationship to the whole.

———————— ————————

The man who is clear and simple does not choose. What is, is. Action based on an idea is obviously the action of choice and such action is not liberating. On the contrary, it creates further resistance, further conflict. Assume pliable awareness.

———————— ————————

Relationship is understanding. It is a process of self-revelation. Relationship is the mirror in which you discover yourself — to be is to be related.

———————— ————————

Set patterns, incapable of adaptability, of pliability, only offer a better cage. Truth is outside of all patterns.

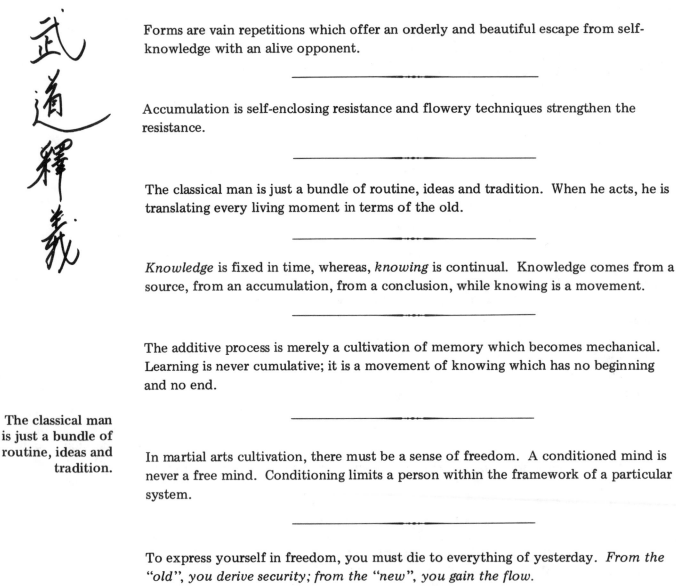

Forms are vain repetitions which offer an orderly and beautiful escape from self-knowledge with an alive opponent.

――――――――――――――

Accumulation is self-enclosing resistance and flowery techniques strengthen the resistance.

――――――――――――――

The classical man is just a bundle of routine, ideas and tradition. When he acts, he is translating every living moment in terms of the old.

――――――――――――――

Knowledge is fixed in time, whereas, *knowing* is continual. Knowledge comes from a source, from an accumulation, from a conclusion, while knowing is a movement.

――――――――――――――

The additive process is merely a cultivation of memory which becomes mechanical. Learning is never cumulative; it is a movement of knowing which has no beginning and no end.

――――――――――――――

The classical man is just a bundle of routine, ideas and tradition.

In martial arts cultivation, there must be a sense of freedom. A conditioned mind is never a free mind. Conditioning limits a person within the framework of a particular system.

――――――――――――――

To express yourself in freedom, you must die to everything of yesterday. *From the "old", you derive security; from the "new", you gain the flow.*

――――――――――――――

To realize freedom, the mind has to learn to look at life, which is a vast movement without the bondage of time, for freedom lies beyond the field of consciousness. Watch, but don't stop and interpret, "I am free" — then you're living in a memory of something that has gone. To understand and live *now*, everything of yesterday must die.

――――――――――――――

Freedom from knowing is death; then, you are living. Die inwardly of "pro" and "con." There is no such thing as doing right or wrong when there is freedom.

――――――――――――――

When one is not expressing himself, he is not free. Thus, he begins to struggle and the struggle breeds methodical routine. Soon, he is doing his methodical routine as response rather than responding to what *is*.

The fighter is to always be single-minded with one object in view — to fight, looking neither backward nor sideways. He must get rid of obstructions to his forward movement, emotionally, physically or intellectually.

One can function freely and totally if he is "beyond system." The man who is really serious, with the urge to find out what truth is, has no style at all. He lives only in what is.

If you want to understand the truth in martial arts, to see any opponent clearly, you must throw away the notion of styles or schools, prejudices, likes and dislikes, and so forth. Then, your mind will cease all conflict and come to rest. In this silence, you will see totally and freshly.

If any style teaches you a method of fighting, then you might be able to fight according to the limit of that method, but that is not actually fighting.

If you meet the unconventional attack, such as one delivered with broken rhythm, with your chosen patterns of rhythmical classical blocks, your defense and counter-attack will always be lacking pliability and aliveness.

If you follow the classical pattern, you are understanding the routine, the tradition, the shadow — you are not understanding yourself.

How can one respond to the totality with partial, fragmentary pattern?

Mere repetition of rhythmic, calculated movements robs combat movement of its "aliveness" and "isness" — its reality.

Accumulation of forms, just one more modification of conditioning, becomes an anchor that holds and ties down; it leads only one way — down.

If you follow the classical pattern, you are understanding the routine, the tradition, the shadow — you are not understanding yourself.

17

Form is the cultivation of resistance; it is the exclusive drilling of a pattern of choice moves. Instead of creating resistance, enter straight into the movement as it arises; do not condemn or condone — choiceless awareness leads to reconciliation with the opponent in a total understanding of what is.

———————

Once conditioned in a partialized method, once isolated in an enclosing pattern, the practitioner faces his opponent through a screen of resistance — he is "performing" his stylized blocks and listening to his own screaming and not seeing what the opponent is really doing.

———————

We are those kata, we are those classical blocks and thrusts, so heavily conditioned are we by them.

———————

To fit in with an opponent one needs direct perception. There is no direct perception where there is a resistance, a "this is the only way" attitude.

———————

Truth has no path. Truth is living and, therefore, changing.

Having *totality* means being capable of following "what is," because "what is" is constantly moving and constantly changing. If one is anchored to a particular view, one will not be able to follow the swift movement of "what is."

———————

Whatever one's opinion of hooking and swinging as part of one's style, there cannot be the least argument to acquiring perfect defenses against it. Indeed, nearly all natural fighters use it. As for the martial artist, it adds versatility to his attack. He must be able to hit from wherever his hand is.

———————

But in classical styles, *system* becomes more important than the man! The classical man functions with the pattern of a style!

———————

How can there be methods and systems to arrive at something that is living? To that which is static, fixed, dead, there can be a way, a definite path, but not to that which is living. Do not reduce reality to a static thing and then invent methods to reach it.

———————

Truth is relationship with the opponent; constantly moving, living, never static.

———————

Truth has no path. Truth is living and, therefore, changing. It has no resting place, no form, no organized institution, no philosophy. When you see that, you will understand that this living thing is also what you are. You cannot express and be alive through static, put-together form, through stylized movement.

Classical forms dull your creativity, condition and freeze your sense of freedom. You no longer "be," but merely "do," without sensitivity.

Just as yellow leaves may be gold coins to stop the crying children, thus, the so-called secret moves and contorted postures appease the unknowledgeable martial artists.

This does not mean to do nothing at all, but only to have no deliberate mind in whatever one does. Do not have a mind that selects or rejects. To be without deliberate mind is to hang no thoughts.

Acceptance, denial and conviction prevent understanding. Let your mind move together with another's in understanding with sensitivity. Then, there is a possibility of real communication. To understand one another, there must be a state of choiceless awareness where there is no sense of comparison or condemnation, no waiting for a further development of discussion in order to agree or disagree. *Above all, don't start from a conclusion.*

> Awareness is without choice, without demand, without anxiety; in that state of mind, there is perception.

Understand the freedom from the conformity of styles. Free yourself by observing closely what you normally practice. Do not condemn or approve; merely observe.

When you are uninfluenced, when you die to the conditioning of classical responses, then you will know awareness and see things totally fresh, totally new.

Awareness is without choice, without demand, without anxiety; in that state of mind, there is perception. Perception alone will resolve all our problems.

Understanding requires not just a moment of perception, but a continuous awareness, a continuous state of inquiry without conclusion.

To understand combat, one must approach it in a very simple and direct manner.

武
道
釋
義

Understanding comes about through feeling, from moment to moment in the mirror of relationship.

———————————————————

Understanding oneself happens through a process of relationships and not through isolation.

———————————————————

To know oneself is to study oneself in action with another person.

———————————————————

To understand the actual requires awareness, an alert and totally free mind.

———————————————————

Effort within the mind further limits the mind, because effort implies struggle towards a goal and when you have a goal, a purpose, an end in view, you have placed a limit on the mind.

———————————————————

To know oneself is to study oneself in action with another person.

This evening I see something totally new and that newness is experienced by the mind, but tomorrow that experience becomes mechanical if I try to repeat the sensation, the pleasure of it. The description is never real. What is real is seeing the truth instantaneously, because truth has no tomorrow.

———————————————————

We shall find the truth when we examine the problem. The problem is never apart from the answer. The problem *is* the answer — understanding the problem dissolves the problem.

———————————————————

Observe what *is* with undivided awareness.

———————————————————

True thusness is without defiling thought; it cannot be known through conception and thought.

———————————————————

Thinking is not freedom — all thought is partial; it can never be total. Thought is the response of memory and memory is always partial, because memory is the result of experience. So, thought is the reaction of a mind conditioned by experience.

Know the emptiness and tranquility of your mind. Be empty; have no style or form for the opponent to work on.

The mind is originally without activity; the way is always without thought.

Insight is realizing that one's original nature is not created.

There will be calmness, tranquility, when one is free from external objects and is not perturbed. Being tranquil means not having any illusions or delusions of thusness.

There is no thought, only thusness — what is. Thusness does not move, but its motion and function are inexhaustible.

To meditate means to realize the imperturbability of one's original nature. Surely, meditation can never be a process of concentration, because the highest form of thinking is negation. Negation is a state in which there is neither the positive, nor its reaction as the negative. It is a state of complete emptiness.

> Awareness has no frontier; it is a giving of your whole being, without exclusion.

Concentration is a form of exclusion and where there is exclusion, there is a thinker who excludes. It is the thinker, the excluder, the one who concentrates, who creates contradiction because he forms a center from which there is distraction.

There is a state of action without the actor, a state of experiencing without the experiencer or the experience. It is a state bound and weighted down by the classical mess.

Classical concentration that focuses on one thing and excludes all others, and awareness, which is total and excludes nothing, are states of the mind that can be understood only by objective, non-prejudiced observation.

Awareness has no frontier; it is a giving of your whole being, without exclusion.

Concentration is a narrowing down of the mind. But we are concerned with the total process of living and to concentrate exclusively on any particular aspect of life, belittles life.

The "moment" has not yesterday or tomorrow. It is not the *result* of thought and, therefore, has not time.

When, in a split second, your life is threatened, do you say, "Let me make sure my hand is on my hip, and my style is 'the' style"? When your life is in danger, do you argue about the method you will adhere to while saving yourself? Why the duality?

A so-called martial artist is the result of three thousand years of propaganda and conditioning.

Self-expression is total, immediate, without conception of time, and you can only express that if you are free, physically and mentally, from fragmentation.

Why do individuals depend on thousands of years of propaganda? They may preach "softness" as the ideal to "firmness," but when "what is" hits, what happens? Ideals, principles, the "what should be" leads to hypocrisy.

Because one does not want to be disturbed, to be made uncertain, he establishes a pattern of conduct, of thought, a pattern of relationships to man. He then becomes a slave to the pattern and takes the pattern to be the real thing.

Agreeing to certain patterns of movement to secure the participants within the governed rules might be good for sports like boxing or basketball, but the success of Jeet Kune Do lies in its freedom, both to use technique and to dispense with it.

The second-hand artist blindly following his sensei or sifu accepts his pattern. As a result, his action and, more importantly, his thinking become mechanical. His responses become automatic, according to set patterns, making him narrow and limited.

Self-expression is total, immediate, without conception of time, and you can only express that if you are free, physically and mentally, from fragmentation.

THE FACTS OF JEET KUNE DO

1. The economy-tight structure in attack and defense
   (attack: the alive leads / defense: sticking hands).
2. The versatile and "artless-artful," "total" kicking and striking weapons.
3. The broken rhythm, the half-beat and the one or three-and-a-half beat
   (JKD's rhythm in attack and counter).
4. Weight training and scientific supplementary training plus all-around fitness.
5. The "JKD direct movement" in attacks and counters — throwing from where it
   is without repositioning.
6. The shifty body and light footwork.
7. The "un-crispy" stuff and unassuming attacking tactics.
8. Strong in-fighting — a. shifty blasting
   b. throwing
   c. grappling
   d. immobilizations
9. All-out sparring and the actual contact training on moving targets.
10. The sturdy tools through continuous sharpening.
11. Individual expression rather than mass product; aliveness rather than classicalism
    (true relationship).
12. *Total* rather than partial in structure.
13. The training of "continuity of expressive self" behind physical movements.
14. Loose power and powerful thrust-drive as a whole. A springy looseness but not a
    physically lax body. Also, a pliable mental awareness.
15. The constant flow (straight movement and curved movement combined — up and
    down, curved left and right, sidesteps, bobbing and weaving, hand circles).
16. Well-balanced posture of exertion during movement, constantly. Continuity be-
    tween near all-out and near all-loose.

I hope martial artists are more interested in the root of martial arts and not the different decorative branches, flowers or leaves.

THE FORMLESS FORM

I hope martial artists are more interested in the root of martial arts and not the different decorative branches, flowers or leaves. It is futile to argue as to which single leaf, which design of branches or which attractive flower you like; when you understand the root, you understand all its blossoming.

Please do not be concerned with soft versus firm, kicking versus striking, grappling versus hitting and kicking, long-range fighting versus in-fighting. There is no such thing as "this" is better than "that." Should there be one thing we must guard against, let it be partiality that robs us of our pristine wholeness and makes us lose unity in the midst of duality.

In combative arts, it has been the problem of ripening. This ripening is the progressive integration of the individual with his being, his essence. This is possible only through self-exploration in free expression, and not in imitative repetition of an imposed pattern of movement.

There are styles that favor straight lines, then there are styles that favor curved lines and circles. Styles that cling to one partial aspect of combat are in bondage. Jeet Kune Do is a technique for acquiring liberty; it is a work of enlightenment. Art is never decoration or embellishment. A choice method, however exacting, fixes its practitioners in a pattern. Combat is never fixed and is changing from moment to moment. Working in patterns is basically a practice of resistance. Such practice leads to clogginess; understanding is not possible and its adherents are never free.

The way of combat is not based on personal choice and fancies. Truth in the way of combat is perceived from moment to moment and only when there is awareness without condemnation, justification or any form of identification.

The height of cultivation runs to simplicity. Half-way cultivation runs to ornamentation.

Jeet Kune Do favors formlessness so that it can assume all forms and, since it has no style, Jeet Kune Do fits in with all styles. As a result, Jeet Kune Do uses all ways and is bound by none and, likewise, uses any technique or means which serves its end. In this art, efficiency is anything that scores.

The height of cultivation runs to simplicity. Half-way cultivation runs to ornamentation.

It is not difficult to trim and hack off the non-essentials in outward physical structure; however, to shun away, to minimize inwardly is another matter.

You cannot see a street fight in its totality, observing it from the viewpoint of a boxer, a kung-fu man, a karateka, a wrestler, a judo man and so forth. You can see clearly only when style does not interfere. You then see it without "like" or "dislike;" you simply see and what you see is the whole and not the partial.

There is "what is" only when there is no comparing and to live with "what is" is to be peaceful.

Fighting is not something dictated by your conditioning as a kung-fu man, a karate man, a judo man or what not. And seeking the opposite of a system is to enter another conditioning.

A Jeet Kune Do man faces reality and not crystallization of form. The tool is a tool of formless form.

No abode means that the ultimate source of all things is beyond human understanding, beyond the categories of time and space. As it thus transcends all modes of relativity, it is called "having no abode" and its qualities are applicable.

The fighter who has no abode is no more himself. He moves as a kind of automaton. He has given himself up to an influence outside his everyday consciousness, which is not other than his own deeply buried unconscious, whose presence he was never hitherto aware of.

Expression is not developed through the practice of form, yet form is a *part* of expression. The greater (expression) is not found in the lesser (expression) but the lesser is found within the greater. Having "no form," then, does not mean having no "form." Having "no form" evolves from having form. "No form" is the higher, individual expression.

A Jeet Kune Do man faces reality and not crystallization of form. The tool is a tool of formless form.

No cultivation does not really mean the absence of any kind of cultivation. What it signifies is a cultivation by means of non-cultivation. To practice cultivation through cultivation is to act with conscious mind. That is to say, to practice assertive activity.

Do not deny the classical approach simply as a reaction, for you will have created another pattern and trapped yourself there.

The physically bound go for puffing and straining and miss the delicate way; the intellectually bound go for idealism and exotics and lack efficiency and actually seeing into realities.

Many a martial artist likes "more," likes "something different," not knowing the truth and the way is exhibited in the simple everyday movements, *because* it is *here* they miss it. If there is any secret, it is missed by seeking.

PRELIMINARIES

To become different from what we are, we must have some awareness of what we are.

TRAINING

Training is one of the most neglected phases of athletics. Too much time is given to the development of skill and too little to the development of the individual for participation. Training deals not with an object, but with the *human spirit* and *human emotions.* It takes intellect and judgment to handle such delicate qualities as these.

———————————————

Training is the *psychological* and *physiological* conditioning of an individual preparing for intense neural and muscular reaction. It implies discipline of the mind and power and endurance of the body. It means skill. It is all these things working together in harmony.

———————————————

Training means not only knowledge of the things which will build the body, but also knowledge of the things which will tear down or injure the body. Improper training will result in injuries. Training, then, is concerned with the prevention of injuries as well as first-aid to injuries.

———————————————

Fitness Program

1) Alternate Splits
2) Push-ups
3) Running in Place
4) Shoulder Circling
5) High Kicks
6) Deep Knee Bends
7) Side Kick Raises
8) Twisting Sit-ups
9) Waist Twisting
10) Leg Raises
11) Forward Bends

Training deals not with an object, but with the human spirit and human emotions.

———————————————

Everyday opportunities for exercises

\#   Take a walk whenever you can — like parking the car a few blocks away from your destination.

\#   Avoid taking the elevator; climb the stairs instead.

\#   Cultivate your quiet awareness by imagining an opponent attacking you — while you are sitting, standing, or lying down, etc. — and counter that attack with various moves. Simple moves are the best.

\#   Practice your balance by standing on one foot to put your clothes or shoes on — or simply stand on one foot whenever you choose.

Supplementary Training

(1) Sequence Training:

        sequence 1 (Mon. Wed. Fri.)

1)	Rope jumping	4)	Jumping jack
2)	Forward bend	5)	Squat
3)	Cat stretch	6)	High kick

        sequence 2 (Tues. Th. Sat.)

1)	Groin stretch	4)	Shoulder circling
2)	Side leg raise	5)	Alternate splits
3)	Jumping squat	6)	Leg stretch — A,B.

(2) Forearm/Waist:

        sequence 1 (Mon. Wed. Fri.)

1)	Waist twisting	4)	Knee drawing
2)	Palm up curl	5)	Side bend
3)	Roman chair	6)	Palm down curl

        sequence 2 (Tues. Th. Sat.)

1)	Leg raises	4)	Leverage bar twist
2)	Reverse curl	5)	Alternate leg raise
3)	Sit-up twist	6)	Wrist roller

(3) Power Training:

1)	Press lockout	4)	Pull	7)	Deadlift
2)	Press start	5)	Squat	8)	Quarter squat
3)	Rise on toes	6)	Shrug	9)	Frog kick

A rehearsal of the skill before competition commences fixes in the athlete's neuromuscular coordinating system the exact nature of the impending task.

WARMING UP

Warming up is a process which elicits the acute physiological changes that prepare the organism for strenuous physical performance.

IMPORTANT: To gain the greatest benefit from the warming-up procedure, the exercises should imitate as closely as possible the movements which are to be used in the event.

Warming up reduces the viscosity of a muscle, its resistance to its own movement. It improves performance and prevents injury in vigorous activities by two essential means:

1. A rehearsal of the skill before competition commences fixes in the athlete's *neuromuscular coordinating system* the exact nature of the impending task. It also *heightens his kinesthetic senses.*

2. The rise in body temperature facilitates the *biochemical reactions supplying*

energy for muscular contractions. Elevated body temperature also shortens the periods of *muscular relaxation* and aids in *reducing stiffness.*

As a result of these two processes, there is an improvement in accuracy, strength and speed of movement, and an increase in *tissue elasticity* which lessens the liability to injury.

No fighter uses his leg violently until he warms it up carefully. The same principle is equally applicable to any muscles that are to be used so vigorously.

The duration of the warm-up period varies with the event. In ballet, the dancers spend two hours before the performance, commencing with very light movements and gradually increasing the intensity and range of motions until the moment before their appearance. This, they feel, reduces the risk of a pulled muscle which would destroy the perfection of their movements.

The athlete of more advanced years tends to warm up more slowly and for a longer time. This fact may be due to greater need for a longer warm-up period, or it may be because an athlete tends to get "smarter" as he gets older.

Indian Wrestling exercises

THE BAITHAK (SQUAT)   THE DAND (CAT-STRETCH)

Proper posture is a matter of effective interior organization of the body.

ON-GUARD POSITION

Proper posture is a matter of effective interior organization of the body which can be achieved only by long and well-disciplined practice.

The On-guard Position inclined forward a little

(#) naturalness mean (a) easily, and (b) comfortably --- all its muscle can act with the greatest speed and ease

(#) ensures complete muscular freedom

[distinguish between dwelling comfort and personal comfort]   [small phasic bent-knee stance] SPBKS   (a) great sensitivity with awareness   (b) mechanically not hamper

rear heel is cocked — with more weight on it

The on-guard position is that position most favorable to the mechanical execution of all the total techniques and skills. It allows complete relaxation yet, at the same time, gives a muscle tonus most favorable to quick reaction time.

You are never set or tensed, but ready and flexible.

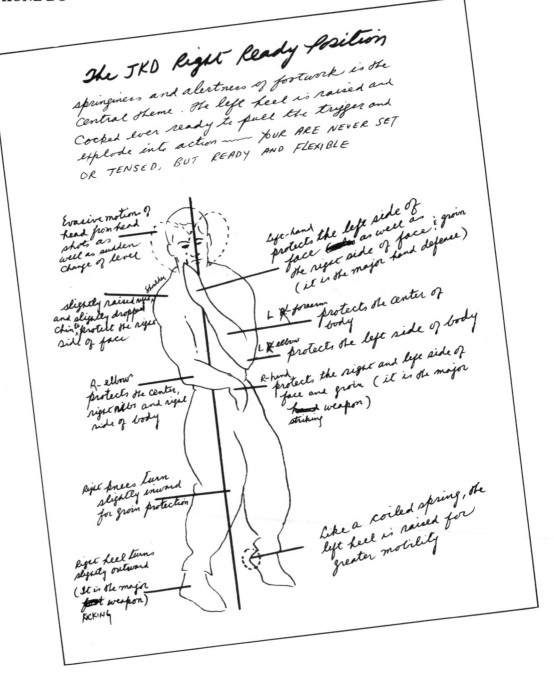

The JKD Right Ready Position

springiness and alertness of footwork is the central theme. The left heel is raised and cocked ever ready to pull the trigger and explode into action —— YOUR ARE NEVER SET OR TENSED, BUT READY AND FLEXIBLE

Evasive motion of head from head shots as well as sudden change of level

slightly raised and slightly dropped chin to protect the right side of face

R-elbow protects the center, right ribs and right side of body

Right knees turn slightly inward for groin protection

Right heel turns slightly outward (It is the major foot weapon) KICKING

Lee-hand protects the left side of face as well as the right side of face & groin (it is the major hand defense)

L forearm protects the center of body

L elbow protects the left side of body

R-hand protects the right and left side of face and groin (it is the major hand striking weapon)

Like a coiled spring, the left heel is raised for greater mobility

A correct posture does three things:

1. It insures for the body and its several members a position which is most mechanically favorable for the next move.

2. It enables one to maintain a "poker body," a body that reveals no more of its intended movements than a "poker face" reveals the cards of a player.

3. It puts the body under that particular tension or degree of tonus which will be most favorable to quick reaction and high coordination.

The JKD Left Ready Position

Springiness and alertness of footwork is the key theme. The right heel is raised and cocked ever ready to pull the trigger into action — YOU ARE NEVER SET OR TENSED, BUT READY AND FLEXIBLE

R-hand protects the right and left side of face and groin (it is the major hand defence)

R-forearm protects the center of body

R-elbow protect the right side of body

Left hand protects the left and right side of face and groin (it is the major striking weapon)

Like a coiled spring, the right heel is raised for greater mobility

Evasive motions of head from head shot — as well as sudden change of level

slightly raised left shoulder and slightly dropped chin to protect the left side of face

Left elbow protects the center, left ribs and left side of body

Left knee turn slightly inward for groin protection

Left heel turn slightly outward (it is the major kicking weapon)

The position adopted should be the one found to give maximum ease and relaxation, combined with smoothness of movement at all times.

The position adopted should be the one found to give maximum ease and relaxation, combined with smoothness of *movement at all times.*

———————————

The on-guard position must, above all, be a "proper spiritual attitude" stance.

———————————

ALTERNATIVE
READY POSITION

The Head

In Western boxing, the head is treated as if it were a part of the trunk, generally, with

no independent action of its own. In close-in fighting, it should be carried vertically, with the point of the chin pinned to the collarbone and the side of the chin held against the inside of the lead shoulder. The chin does not go all the way down to meet the shoulder, nor does the shoulder come all the way up. They meet halfway. The shoulder is raised an inch or two and the chin is dropped an inch or two.

The *point* of the chin is not tucked into the lead shoulder except when angling the head back in an *extreme defensive position*. Tucking the point of the chin into the lead shoulder turns the neck into an unnatural position, takes away the support of the muscles and *prevents straight bone alignment*. It also tenses the lead shoulder and arm, preventing free action and causing fatigue.

With the chin dropped and pinned tight to the collarbone, the muscles and bone structure are in the best possible alignment and only the top of the head is presented to the opponent, making it impossible to be hit on the point of the chin.

The Lead Arm and Hand

> Keep the lead hand always in some subtle motion for easier initiation.

The shoulder is loose and the hand is held slightly lower, relaxed and ready for attacking. The entire arm and shoulder must be loose and relaxed so that the fighter will be able to snap or whip out the lead in rapier-like thrusts. The hand position changes frequently from the low back fist position to about shoulder height and as far to the outside of the lead shoulder as possible without raising the elbow. Keep the lead hand always in some subtle motion for easier initiation.

The preference for a low-line position with absence of an extended lead is because most people are weak in low-line defense. Also, with the absence of an extended lead, many preparations on same are useless. (The head now becomes a moving target, augmented by sensitive distance.) So, if the opponent's offensive game is based on these preparatory movements, he is severely handicapped and partly checked.

The elongated guard can prove a dangerous weakness in both attacks and defense.

In attacks:
1. Necessitates withdrawing the arm, thus telegraphing (unlike a coiled spring).
2. Needs preparation for hooks.

In defense:
1. Uncovers the lead side of the body.
2. The opponent *knows where it is* and can maneuver all around it.
3. An extended hand offers itself for immobilization.

Thus, adopt the recommended position to keep the potentialities of your lead reach a secret.

The Rear Arm and Hand

The rear elbow is held down and in front of the short ribs. The rear forearm covers the solar plexus. The open palm of the rear hand faces the opponent and is positioned between the opponent and the rear shoulder, in line with the lead shoulder. The rear hand may also rest lightly upon the body. The arm should be relaxed and easy, *ready to attack or defend.* Either or both hands may perform a circular "weaving" motion. The important thing is to keep them moving, but retain cover.

The Trunk

The position of the trunk is controlled primarily by the position of the leading foot and leg. If the leading foot and leg are in the correct position, the trunk automatically assumes the proper position. *The one important thing about the trunk is that it should form a straight line with the leading leg.* As the leading foot and leg are turned inward, the body rotates in the same direction, which presents a narrow target to the opponent. If, however, the leading foot and leg are rotated outward, the body is squared toward the opponent, presenting a large target. For defensive purposes, the narrow target is advantageous, while the square position lends itself better to some attacks.

The one important thing about the trunk is that it should form a straight line with the leading leg.

Stance

The semi-crouch stance is the perfect stance for fighting because you are braced but are, at all times, in a comfortably balanced position from which you can attack, counter, or defend *without preliminary movement.* This stance may be referred to as the *"small phasic bent-knee stance."*

> *SMALL:* Means appropriateness, not over-extended steps nor insufficient length of stepping. Small quick steps for speed and controlled balance in bridging gap to opponent, not distinctive enough for opponent to time.

> *PHASIC:* A stage or interval in a development or cycle, not still or static, but constantly changing.

> *BENT-KNEE:* Ensures readiness in motion at all times.

The pattern of bent knees, crouched trunk, slightly forward center of gravity and partially flexed arm is characteristic of "readiness" in many sports.

At any time, the lead foot should be hampered as little as possible. If too much weight is on it, it will be necessary to transfer that weight to the rear leg before starting the attack. This movement involves a *delay* and also *warns* the opponent.

FUNDAMENTAL POSITIONING is the foundation.

Fundamental suggests:
1. Simple but effective organization of oneself mentally and physically.
2. Ease, comfort and body feel during maintenance of the *"spiritual stance."*
3. Simplicity. Movement with no strain. Being neutral, it has no commitment in directional course or exertion.

Positioning suggests:
1. A state of *movement* as opposed to a static position, an "established" form or attitude.
2. Repositioning, especially with small phasic movement, resulting in further disorganization of the opponent's sustained watchfulness.
3. Adaptation to opponent's watchfulness.

Springiness and alertness of footwork is the key theme. The rear heel is raised and cocked, ever ready to pull the trigger into action. *You are never set or tensed, but are ready and flexible.*

Balance is the most important consideration in the on-guard position.

The primary purpose of JKD is kicking, hitting and applying bodily force. Therefore, the use of the on-guard position is to obtain the most favorable position for the above-mentioned.

To hit or to kick effectively, it is necessary to shift weight constantly from one leg to the other. This means perfect control of body balance. *Balance is the most important consideration in the on-guard position.*

Naturalness means *easily* and *comfortably*, so all muscles can act with the greatest speed and ease. Stand loosely and lightly, avoid tension and muscular contraction. *Distinguish between drilling comfort and personal comfort.* Thus, you will both guard and hit with more speed, precision and power.

You are all back, elbows, forearms, fist and forehead. You look more on the order of a cat with its back hunched up and ready to spring, except that you are relaxed. Your opponent hasn't much to shoot at. Your chin is tucked between your shoulders. Your elbows protect your sides. You are partially contracted in the middle. The on-guard position is the safest position.

Thus:
1. Use tools that will least deviate from the on-guard position.

2. Practice instantaneous explosion from neutrality and retain neutrality in commitment, all into one constant smooth flow.
3. Practice constantly to apply *all* tools from the on-guard position and return to the on-guard position with all possible rapidity. Shorten the gap time between position and execution more and more. *Ease*, speed, relay.

Above all, do not lay down restricting rules.

PROGRESSIVE WEAPONS CHARTS

Because of their advanced position, your leading foot and hand constitute at least 80 per cent of all kicking and striking (they are halfway to the target before starting). It

The Right lead stance

Like the Cobra, you remain coiled in a loose but compact position, and your strike should be felt before it is seen

Above all, do not lay down restricting rules.

is important that they can strike with speed and power singly or in combinations. Also, they must be reinforced by equal precision of the rear foot and hand.

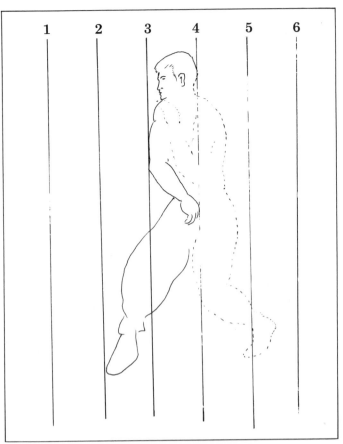

RIGHT LEAD STANCE

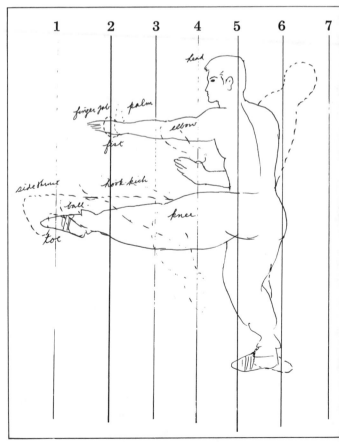

RIGHT LEADING WEAPONS

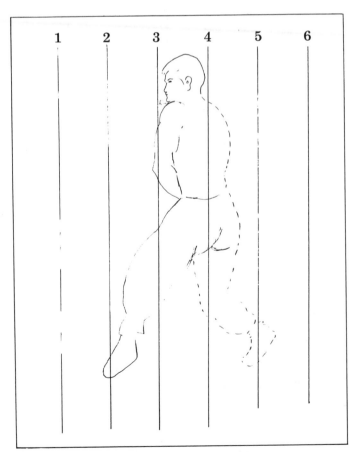

LEFT LEAD STANCE

LEFT LEADING WEAPONS

EIGHT BASIC DEFENSE POSITIONS
(left and right stances)

右擺椿左右手消勢全圖

左擺椿左右手消勢全圖

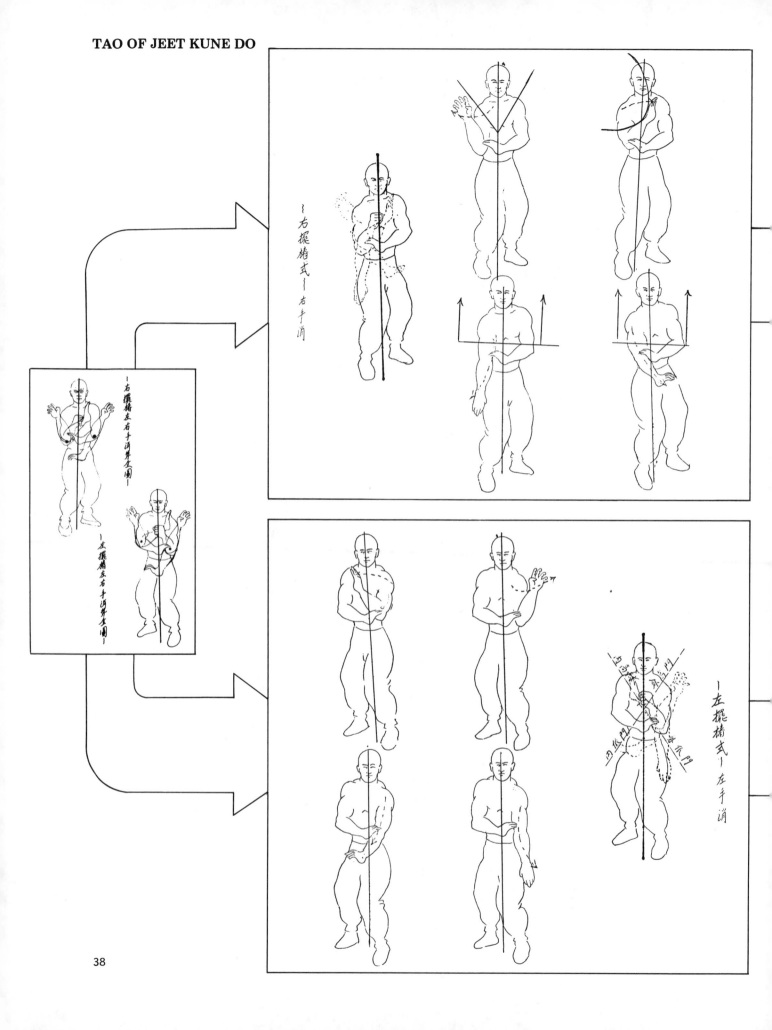

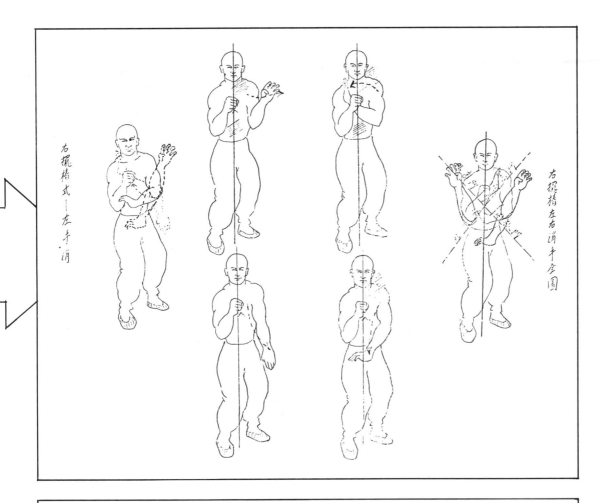

Like the cobra, you remain coiled in a loose but compact position and your strike should be felt before it is seen.

武道釋義

SOME TARGET AREAS

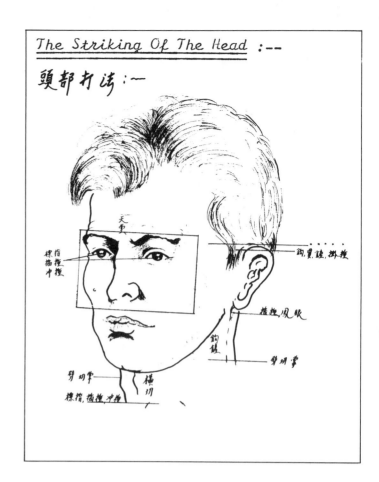

The Striking Of The Head :—

頭部打法:—

詠春派先師秘傳總訣

師曰生死費睿訣須知春夏秋冬四季分十二叶反
方可以斷生死 若不大傷心之事不可行之倘出外往別方
或因路途隱阻倘遇惡人 此手自不可忍亦非惡人何必
傷人之命也 此手出在三尖 何为三尖虎尖掌尖肖尖
定要子午分明百發百中 賢徒單習此手仍須傳師口訣
分明勢力工夫 百中難晚 但使手須善而用之若惱亏
不能成功矢 出手仍雖要虎尖掌尖諸眉尖諸掌尖 切不可
亂傷人命 若亂傷人命是志先師什託之言沒亏良
心也 此書不可亂傳亏義亏信之人紧記 师
有持四句亏:江湖一点訣莫叶親朋睨 若叶亏義說
七吼皆流血 人有十八穴五十四小穴天地八和
四大穴乃傷人之命也 何为小穴手足四股是乃內外
骨節共成七十二穴葉有七十二方單習練成葉可以
治之 若出外往別處 非知心者不可亂言戲語怕
人暗算为人四海見事覓諜为師者紧記紧記—

太極門之八死穴 :—

(1) 曰夫頃　　　　(5) 曰兩肋乳
(2) 曰兩耳　　　　(6) 曰前陰
(3) 曰咽喉　　　　(7) 曰兩腎
(4) 曰中脘　　　　(8) 曰尾閭

螳螂派 八打与八不打

八不打 (死穴) :—

(1) 太陽亏肯　　　(5) 海底撩陰
(2) 正中鎖喉　　　(6) 兩腎叶心
(3) 中心兩壁　　　(7) 尾閭風府
(4) 兩肋太極　　　(8) 兩耳扇風

八打 :—

(1) 眉頭双睛　　　(5) 脅內肺腑
(2) 唇上人中　　　(6) 撩陰高骨頭
(3) 穿腮耳門　　　(7) 鮭腰虎頭
(4) 背後骨縫　　　(8) 破骨十斤

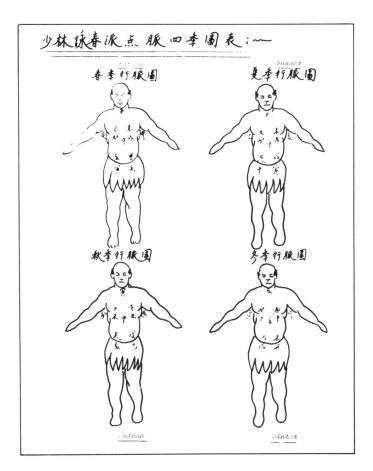

少林詠春派点脈四季圖表:—

春季行脈圖　　夏季行脈圖

秋季行脈圖　　冬季行脈圖

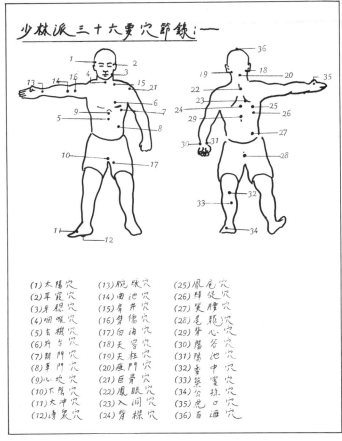

少林派三十六要穴節錄:—

(1) 太陽穴　　(13) 腕咏穴　　(25) 鳳尾穴
(2) 耳寰穴　　(14) 曲池穴　　(26) 精促穴
(3) 身腿穴　　(15) 肩井穴　　(27) 笑腰穴
(4) 咽喉穴　　(16) 肩偏海穴　(28) 尾龜穴
(5) 玄棋穴　　(17) 白海穴　　(29) 背心穴
(6) 胖兮穴　　(18) 天窖穴　　(30) 陽谷穴
(7) 期門穴　　(19) 天柱穴　　(31) 陽池中穴
(8) 軍門穴　　(20) 天雁穴　　(32) 背珠穴
(9) 心坎穴　　(21) 巨骨穴　　(33) 築谷穴
(10) 下陰穴　　(22) 鳳眼穴　　(34) 虎口穴
(11) 太冲穴　　(23) 入洞穴　　(35) 百匯穴
(12) 湧泉穴　　(24) 背楳穴　　(36) 百匯穴

The First Two Primary Targets;

上取眼下撩陰 —

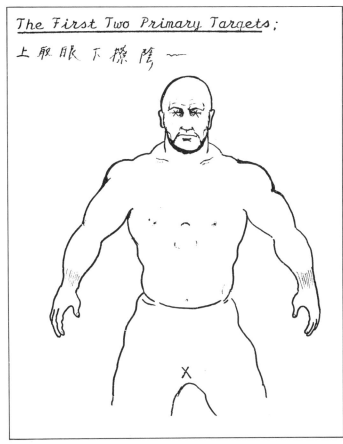

Vital spots of The Body 身體要害

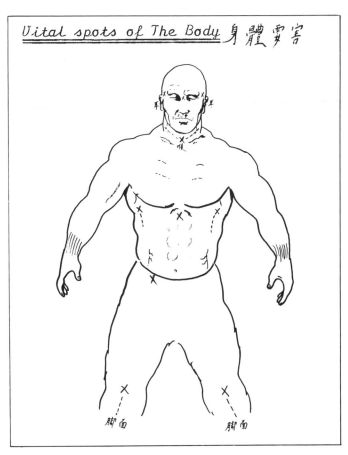

腳面　　　腳面

41

QUALITIES

It's not daily increase but daily decrease—hack away the unessentials!

COORDINATION

Coordination is by all means one of *the* most important considerations in any study of proficiency in sports and athletics. Coordination is the quality which enables the individual to integrate all the powers and capacities of his whole organism into an effective *doing* of an act.

Before movements can take place, there must be a change of muscular tension on both sides of the joints to be moved. The effectiveness of this muscular teamwork is one of the factors which determine limits of speed, endurance, power, agility and accuracy in all athletic performances.

In static or slow resistive activities, such as executing a handstand or supporting a heavy barbell, the muscles on both sides of the joints act strongly to fix the body in the desired position. When rapid motion takes place, as in running or throwing, the muscles closing the joints shorten and those on the opposite side lengthen to permit the movement. There is still tension on both sides, but on the lengthening side, it is considerably reduced.

Any excessive tension in the lengthening muscles acts as a *brake* and thereby slows and weakens the action. Such antagonistic tension increases the energy cost of muscular work, resulting in early fatigue. When a new task with a demand that is different in intensity of load, rate, repetition or duration is undertaken, an entirely new pattern of "neurophysiological adjustment" must be acquired. Thus, the fatigue experienced in new activities is not *just* from using different muscles but is also due to the *braking* caused by improper coordination.

The outstanding characteristic of the expert athlete is his ease of movement, even during maximal effort.

The outstanding characteristic of the expert athlete is his *ease of movement*, even during maximal effort. The novice is characterized by his tenseness, wasted motion and excess effort. That rare person, the "natural athlete," seems to be endowed with the ability to undertake any sport activity, whether he is experienced in it or not, with ease. The *ease* is his ability to perform with *minimal antagonistic tension*. It is more present in some athletes than in others, but can be improved by all.

The fighter whose movements seem awkward, who never seems to find the proper distance, is always being timed, never "out-guesses" his opponent, and always gives warning of his intentions before they become serious, is suffering chiefly from a lack of coordination. The well-coordinated fighter does everything *smoothly* and *gracefully*. He seems to *glide* in and out of distance with a *minimum of effort* and a *maximum of deception*. His timing is usually good because his own movements are so

rhythmical *they tend to establish complementary rhythm* on the part of his opponent, a rhythm he can break to his own advantage because of his perfect control of his own muscles. He seems to out-guess his opponent because he usually *takes the initiative* and, to a large extent, *forces the reactions of his opponent.* Above all, he makes his movements *with a purpose*, rather than with a doubting hope, because he has confidence in himself.

────────────────

Muscles have no power to guide themselves, but the manner in which they act, and consequently the effectiveness of our performances, depends absolutely on how the nervous system guides them. Thus, a badly executed move is the result of impulses sent to the wrong muscles by the nervous system, or sent a fraction of a second too soon or too late, or sent in improper sequence or in poorly apportioned intensity.

────────────────

Well-executed movement means the nervous system *has been trained* to the point where it sends impulses to certain muscles, causing these muscles to contract at exactly the proper fraction of a second. At the same time, impulses to the antagonistic muscles are shut off, allowing those muscles to relax. Properly coordinated impulses surge with just the exact intensity required and they stop at the exact fraction of a second when they are no longer needed.

────────────────

Learning coordination is a matter of training the nervous system and not a question of training muscles.

Therefore, learning coordination is a matter of training the nervous system and not a question of training muscles. The transition from totally uncoordinated muscular effort to skill of the highest perfection is a process of developing the connections in the nervous system. Psychologists and biologists tell us that the billions of elements in the nervous system are not in direct connection with each other, but that the fibers of one nerve cell intertwine with those of other cells in such close proximity that impulses can pass from one to others by a *process of induction.* This point at which the impulse passes from one nerve cell to another is called the *"synapse."* The synapse theory explains why the baby who displayed totally uncoordinated responses at the sight of a ball eventually becomes the big league ball-player.

────────────────

Training for skill (coordination) is purely a matter of forming proper connections in the nervous system through practice (precision practice). Each performance of an act strengthens the connections involved and makes the next performance easier, more certain, and more readily done. Likewise, disuse tends to weaken any pathways that have been formed and makes doing of the act more difficult and uncertain (constant exercises). Thus, we can attain skill only by actually doing the thing we are trying to learn. We learn solely by doing or reacting. When learning to form pathways, be sure the actions are the most economical as well as the most efficient use of energy and motion.

────────────────

To become a champion requires a *condition of readiness* that causes the individual to approach with pleasure even the most tedious practice session. The more "ready" the person is to respond to a stimulus, the more satisfaction he finds in the response, and the more "unready" he is, the more annoying he finds it to be forced to act.

IMPORTANT: Do not practice finely skilled movements after you are tired, for you will begin to *substitute gross motions* for *finer ones* and *generalized efforts* for *specific ones.* Remember, wrong movements tend to supervene and the athlete's progress is set back. *Thus, the athlete practices fine skills only while he is fresh.* When he becomes fatigued, he shifts to tasks employing gross movements designed principally to develop endurance.

PRECISION

Precision of movement means *accuracy* and generally is used in the sense of exactness in the projection of a force.

Precision is made up of controlled body movements. These movements should eventually be executed with a minimum amount of strength and exertion, while still achieving the desired result. Precision can only be attained through a considerable amount of practice and training on the part of *both the beginner and the experienced fighter.*

> Precision of movement means accuracy and generally is used in the sense of exactness in the projection of a force.

Skill is best acquired by learning accuracy and precision first with speed before the skill act is attempted with much *power* and speed.

A mirror is a definite aid to achieving precision by providing a constant check on posture, hand position and technical movement.

POWER

To be accurate, the striking or throwing skills should be executed from a body base that possesses enough strength to maintain adequate balance during the action.

To appropriately incorporate momentum with mechanical advantage, neural impulses are sent to the working muscle to bring a sufficient number of fibers into action at precisely the right time, while impulses to the antagonistic muscles are reduced to lessen the resistance — all acting to improve efficiency and to make the best use of available power.

When approaching an unfamiliar task, the athlete tends to overmobilize his muscular forces, exerting more effort than required. This is a lack of "knowledge" by the reflective neuromuscular coordinating system.

A powerful athlete is not a strong athlete, but one who can exert his strength quickly. Since power equals force times speed, if the athlete learns to make faster movements he increases his power, even though the contractile pulling strength of his muscles remains unchanged. Thus, a smaller man who can swing faster may hit as hard or as far as the heavier man who swings slowly.

The athlete who is building muscles through weight training should be very sure to work adequately on speed and flexibility at the same time. Combined with adequate speed, flexibility and endurance, high levels of strength lead to excellence in most sports. In combat, without the prior attributes, a strong man will be like the bull with its colossal strength futilely pursuing the matador or like a low-geared truck chasing a rabbit.

ENDURANCE

The best form of endurance exercise is the performance of the event.

Endurance is developed by *hard* and *continuous* exercise which exceeds the "steady" physiological state and produces near exhaustion, temporarily. Considerable respiratory and muscular distress should develop.

The best form of endurance exercise is the performance of the event. Of course, running and shadow boxing are necessary supplementary endurance exercises, but you should do them with broken rhythm, broken neurophysiological adjustment.

Most beginning athletes are unwilling to drive themselves hard enough. They should punish themselves and then rest adequately, only to increase the output of effort after the rest. Long hours of work made up of many short, high-speed efforts interspersed with periods of milder activity seem to be the best endurance-training procedure.

Four hypotheses for extra-endurance sports:

1. Endurance can be acquired through a rather extensive succession of sprints interspersed with easier running.
2. One trains for an endurance that is specific to a particular rate of speed.
3. Extreme endurance training should include much more and longer work than what has been customary. (Such "Spartan" training is for the champ.)

4. An occasional change of pace should be included that employs different movements and, to some degree, different muscle fibers.

Exercises for endurance development should be gradually and carefully increased. Six weeks seem to be a scanty minimum for sports that require considerable endurance and six weeks are really only the beginning. The peak of achievement will be approached in years.

Endurance is lost rapidly if one ceases to work at its maintenance.

BALANCE

Balance is the all-important factor in a fighter's attitude or stance. Without balance *at all times*, he can never be effective.

Balance is achieved only through *correct body alignment*. The feet, the legs, the trunk, the head are all important in creating and maintaining a balanced position. They are the vehicles of body force. Keeping the feet in proper relation to each other, as well as to the body, helps to maintain correct body alignment.

Endurance is lost rapidly if one ceases to work at its maintenance.

Too wide a stance prevents proper alignment, destroying the purpose of balance but obtaining solidarity and power at the cost of speed and efficient movement. A short stance prevents balance as it does not give a basis from which to work. Speed results but at a loss of power and balance.

The secret of a proper balance in the proper stance is to keep the feet directly under the body, which means they should be a *medium distance apart*. Either the weight is balanced over both legs or (as in Western boxing) it is carried slightly forward over the lead leg. The lead leg is *fairly* straight and the knee is loose and easy, not locked. The lead side of the body forms a straight line from the lead heel to the tip of the lead shoulder. This position permits relaxation, speed, balance and easy movement, as well as a mechanical advantage, making possible tremendous power.

In general for athletic contests, a preparatory stance will include a "coiled" or semi-crouched posture and a lowered, forward center of gravity. With the bending of the forward knee, the center of gravity moves forward a little. For general readiness, the lead heel usually remains just touching the ground even after the knees bend. Slight ground contact of the heel aids in balance and decreases tension.

Always leave the space of a natural step between your feet. By doing so, you are braced and never standing on just one point.

———————————————

By not getting your feet crossed, you are not likely to be pushed off-balance or knocked down because of bad footwork.

———————————————

Postural habits:

1. Lower the center of gravity.
2. Keep a base with lateral width.
3. Keep weight on the balls of the feet.
4. Knees are rarely straightened, even in running.
5. A center of gravity kept under delicate and rapid motion are characteristic habits of athletes in games that require sudden and frequent changes of direction.

In general for athletic contests, a preparatory stance will include a "coiled" or semi-crouched posture and a lowered, forward center of gravity.

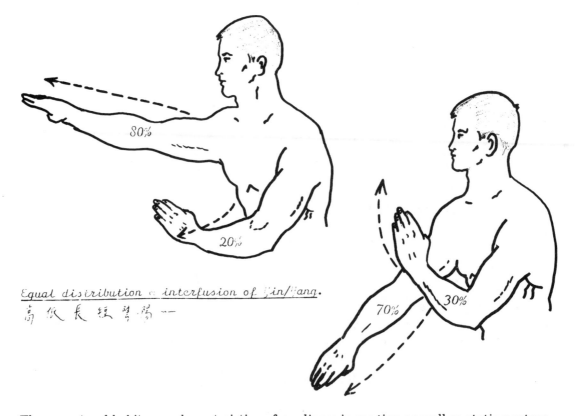

Equal distribution & interfusion of Yin/Yang.

These postural habits are characteristics of *readiness in motion* as well as *static posture.* The athlete displays these static and phasic motor habits before and immediately after each act, in preparation for the next act. When sudden movement may be necessary, the good athlete is rarely caught with a straight knee or with other completely straightened joint angles. From such bent-knee preparatory-running has come the well-known statement, "The good athlete always runs as if his pants need pressing."

Balance is the *control* of one's center of gravity plus the *control* and utilization of body slants and unstable equilibrium, hence gravity pull, to facilitate movement. *So, balance might mean being able to throw one's center of gravity beyond the base of support, chase it, and never let it get away.*

———————————

The *short step* and the *glide*, as contrasted with the hop or cross step, are devices to keep the center of gravity. When it is necessary to move rapidly, the good man takes small enough steps so that his center of gravity is rarely out of control.

———————————

Body slants in a preparatory position are counter-balanced with an extended arm, leg or both.

———————————

One should seek good balance *in motion* and not in stillness.

———————————

The fighter's center of gravity changes constantly, varying with his own actions and *those of his opponent.*

———————————

One should seek good balance in motion and not in stillness.

The missing of a blow or intended kick means momentary loss of balance. That is why the counter-fighter usually has the advantage, but the attacker will be fairly safe by adopting the *small phasic bent-knee stance.* Practice counters the moment your opponent loses his balance, especially if he is the stand-up type.

———————————

Balance must be under control *at all times* so that the fighter will not lose his control in the middle of an action.

\#   For an attack, the center of gravity should imperceptibly be shifted to the front foot in order to allow the back leg and foot freedom for the shortest, fastest and most explosive lunge.

\#   For a parry, the center of gravity should be shifted slightly to the rear foot so that the distance is increased and more time is allowed for the parry and riposte movements.

Always stay in balance to throw another kick or punch. Watch out for too much commitment.

Training Aids

Feel for the proper relation of the feet to each other and to the body while attacking in combination, retreating and countering. Note their positioning for all types of hits and kicks.

Feel yourself in a balanced stance. You should be able to make all your moves at walking pace if necessary. *Feel* the difference by putting yourself in balanced and unbalanced positions. Move forward, backward and sideways. *Coordinate* with striking and kicking; make sure you get speed and power and, above all, a balanced position to keep up or to speedily recover.

One of the finest exercises for the development of a sense of balance is undoubtedly *not* ordinary haphazard skipping, but rather the real thing. First, skip on one foot, holding the other in front of you; then skip on the other. After that, skip on alternate feet with each revolution of the rope (not as simple as it may appear) and work up to the highest possible speed. Keep the skipping going for three minutes (the duration of a round), then rest for a minute and skip for another three minutes. Three rounds of skipping in a variety of ways will form the opening for a good workout.

You should be able to make all your moves at walking pace if necessary.

BODY FEEL

Body Feel suggests a harmonious interplay of body and spirit, both inseparable.

Body Feel in Attack
PHYSICAL:

1. Consider balance before, during, after.
2. Consider air-tight defense before, during, after.
3. Learn to cut into the opponent's moving tools and limit the ground for his agility.
4. Consider aliveness.

MENTAL:

1. Allow the "wanting" to score the target.
2. Back yourself by alertness, awareness to sudden change to defense or counter.
3. Keep a neutral watchfulness at all times, always observing the opponent's actions and reactions to fit in.

4. Learn to relay destructiveness (looseness, speed, compactness, ease) to moving targets.

Body Feel in Defense

1. Study the opponent's delivering method — signs of telegraphing.
2. Learn to time the opponent's second, third moves — read his style and solve the problem should simple attacks fail.
3. Read the opponent's moment of helplessness.
4. Take advantage of a common tendency to "reach" with spent tools.
5. Draw the opponent off balance into one's sensitive aura while keeping your own balance.
6. Be able to express efficiency while moving backward and experiment with all possibilities (sidestepping, curving, etc.). Stay in balance for finishing blows and kicks.
7. At the right moment, attack instantaneously with
    a. correct self-synchronization
    As one b. right distance
    c. right timing

GOOD FORM

Good form is the most efficient manner to accomplish the purpose of a performance with a *minimum of lost motion and wasted energy.*

Body Feel suggests a harmonious interplay of body and spirit, both inseparable.

To conserve energy by using the least possible amount of energy to achieve a given result, eliminate the *unnecessary motions* and *muscle contractions* which fatigue without accomplishing any useful purpose.

The education of neuromuscular skill:

\#   The first step is to acquire the *feeling of relaxation.*
\#   The second step is to practice until this *feeling* can be reproduced at will.
\#   The third step is to reproduce that *feeling* voluntarily in potentially tension-creating situations.

The ability to feel contraction and relaxation, to know what a muscle is doing, is called *"kinesthetic perception."* Kinesthetic perception is developed by consciously placing the body and its parts in a given position and *getting the feel of it.* This feeling of balance or imbalance, grace or awkwardness, serves as a constant guide to the body as it moves.

Kinesthetic perception should be developed to such a degree that the body is uncomfortable unless it performs each motion with a minimum of effort to produce maximum results (apply to posture, too).

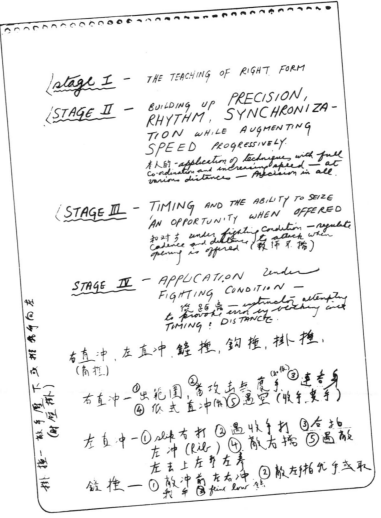

Good form is the most efficient manner to accomplish the purpose of a performance with a minimum of lost motion and wasted energy.

Relaxation is a physical state, but it is controlled by the mental state. It is acquired by the conscious effort to control the *thought* as well as the *action pattern*. It takes *perception*, *practice* and *willingness* to train the mind into new habits of thinking and the body into new habits of action.

Relaxation refers to the degree of tension in the musculature. The rule in sports is to try to have no more tension in the acting muscles than is necessary to perform the act, and to have as low a degree of tension in the antagonistic muscles as possible and still maintain any necessary inhibitory control. Muscles are always in a slight state of tension and this is as they should be. But when they begin to "tighten up" too much, we find our speed and skill being handicapped. The main difficulty in such cases lies in the over tension of the antagonistic muscles. A low degree of tension in the acting muscles means less energy usage. Tense antagonistic muscles waste energy and cause stiffness and/or resistance to the movement. In coordinated, graceful and efficient movement, the opposing muscles must be able to relax and lengthen readily and easily.

Relaxation in sports depends upon the cultivation of mental poise and emotional control. A relaxed technician expends mental and physical energy *constructively*, converting it when it does not contribute to the solution of the problem and spending it freely when it does. It does not mean he is lax and moves and thinks slowly. Neither does it mean he is careless or indifferent. The relaxation desired is *relaxation of muscles, rather than of mind or attention.*

Energy saved by *sound mechanics of form* can be utilized in the *longer persistence* or the *more forceful expression* of the skill.

The older athlete regards form as a means of energy conservation and the great athlete saves energy because his extra skill makes each motion more effective — he makes fewer needless motions and his conditioned body uses less energy per movement.

Always *train in good form.* Learn to move easily and smoothly. Start your workout with shadow boxing to loosen your muscles. At first concentrate on proper form; later, work harder.

> Energy saved by sound mechanics of form can be utilized in the longer persistence or the more forceful expression of the skill.

The mastery of proper fundamentals and their progressive application is the secret of being a great fighter.

In most cases, the same tactic for each maneuver must be drilled on the opposite side of the body for the proper balance in efficiency, but the chief consideration in developing form is to make sure that no fundamental, mechanical principles are violated.

Economy of Motion

There is a best way to perform any task. A few of the principles that have been found to be of importance in improving performance are as follows:

1. Momentum should be employed to overcome resistance.
2. Momentum should be reduced to a minimum if it must be overcome by muscular effort.
3. Continuous *curved motions* require less effort than straight line motions involving sudden and sharp changes in direction.

4. When the initiating muscles are unopposed, allowing free and smooth motion, the movements are faster, easier and more accurate than restricted or controlled movements.

5. Work arranged to permit an easy and natural rhythm is conducive to smooth and automatic performance.

6. Hesitation or the temporary and often minute cessation of motion should be eliminated from the performance.

It is all right to change one's style to adapt to various circumstances, but remember not to change your basic form. By changing style, I mean switching your plan of attack.

Good form may be defined as the particular technique which enables the individual to attain maximum efficiency in the activity.

Good form may be defined as the particular technique which enables the individual to attain maximum efficiency in the activity.

Balance, too, is vital to good form. Whether it be a kick or a punch that you are throwing, you will not have sustained power unless your balance and perfect timing give you enough leverage.

Above all things, remember this: If you tighten up, you lose the flexibility and timing which are so important to successful fighters. Therefore, consciously practice economical neuromuscular perceptive movements *daily* and keep relaxed at all times.

VISION AWARENESS

Learning great speed in *visual recognition* is a basic beginning. Your training should include short, concentrated, daily practice in seeing quickly (awareness drills).

High levels of perceptual speed are the product of learning, not of inheritance.

A boy who is a little slow in reaction time, or in speed of delivery, may compensate for this slowness through quick seeing.

Speed of perception is somewhat affected by the distribution of the observer's attention — fewer separate choices, faster action. When the cue to be recognized is likely to be one of several, each of which requires a different response, the time is lengthened. *Choice reaction takes longer than simple reaction.* This is the basis for training the tools in terms of *neurophysiological adjustment* toward *instinctive economy.* Instinctive movement, being the simplest, is the quickest and most accurate.

Progression from volition to *reflex control* is when an athlete's awareness is shifted from small details (mechanical performance) to larger ones, and finally to the whole action, without a thought given to any single part.

A habit of diffusing the attention over a wider area helps the offensive passer to see openings more quickly.

For most rapid perception, *attention* must be at its maximum focus on the area of the thing to be perceived (i.e.: "Get-set!" takes advantage over an opponent who lacks this "get-set" preparation).

Experiments indicate that auditory cues, when occurring close to the athlete, are responded to more quickly than visual ones. Make use of auditory cues together with visual cues, if possible. Remember, however, the focus of attention on *general movement* produces faster action than focus on hearing or seeing the cue.

High levels of perceptual speed are the product of learning, not of inheritance.

Train yourself to cut down unnecessary choice-reactions (minimize yourself naturally) while giving your opponent a variety of possible responses.

A good man is continually trying to force his opponent into the slower, choice-reaction situation.

Strategies of distracting attention (fakes and feints) are athletic devices to direct the opponent's attention and to make him hesitate before he can be sure of his cue to act. Of course, an additional advantage is gained if the opponent can be induced to make a preliminary motion in an appropriate direction.

The offensive opponent who can hit or kick only from one side permits the defensive opponent the faster action of a one-sided focus of attention.

A person reacts to a quick motion toward his eyes by instinctively blinking. Such instinctive blinking must be controlled in practice or else the opponent, if aware that

the fighter closes his eyes when threatened, may provoke this reaction and utilize the moment of blindness for a hit or kick.

Central vision means that the eyes and attention are fixed on one point. In *peripheral vision*, although the eyes are fixed on one point, the attention is expanded to a larger field. Central vision may be thought of as being sharp and clear, while peripheral vision is more diffuse.

In combat, a student must learn to expand his attention over the entire area by making full use of his peripheral vision.

Exercise: The teacher extends his index finger and instructs his student to concentrate on the point of the finger. He then begins moving the index finger of his other hand into the student's field of vision and slowly describes letters and numerals with it. The student should be able to expand his attention sufficiently to recognize the figures without changing the focus of his eyes.

A good man is continually trying to force his opponent into the slower choice-reaction situation.

The field of vision is enlarged by distance and diminished at close-range. Also, it is generally easier to follow the opponent's footwork than his hand work, since the foot moves relatively slowly compared to the more rapidly moving hand.

The fighter's visual field.

SPEED

Types of speed:

1. **Perceptual speed.** Quickness of eye to see openings and to discourage the opponent, confusing him and slowing him down.

2. **Mental speed.** Quickness of mind to select the right move to frustrate and counter the opponent.

3. **Initiation speed.** Economical starting from the right posture and with the correct mental attitude.

4. **Performance speed.** Quickness of movement in carrying the chosen move into effect. Involves actual muscle contraction speed.

5. **Alteration speed.** The ability to change direction midstream. Involves control of balance and inertia. (Use small phasic bent-knee stance.)

Desirable characteristics to promote speed:

1. Mobility
2. Spring, resilience, elasticity
3. Resistance to fatigue (i.e.: stamina and physical fitness)
4. Physical and mental alertness
5. Imagination and anticipation

Exercises which increase skill and flexibility of both hand and footwork are indispensable building blocks for the fighter. Many fighters fail to appreciate how much true speed depends on *economy of motion* (i.e.: good form and good coordination). Thus, constant mechanical drill (practicing the activity) is essential. A certain amount of *emotional stimulation* helps as well.

Overall tension and unnecessary muscular contractions act as brakes, reducing speed and dissipating energy.

Shadow boxing is a good agility exercise as well as a method for building up speed. Keep your mind on the job! Imagine that your worst enemy, if you happen to have one, is there in front of you and go out to give him all you've got. Use your imagination to the utmost; try to anticipate the moves your phantom rival will endeavor to put across and work yourself up into a real fighting frame of mind. Shadow boxing helps wind, speed, gives ideas and helps the mind fix boxing moves ready for use when they are most wanted.

Economy of form and relaxing the muscles add to speed. One of the greatest adjustments the novice athlete must make in competition is to overcome the natural tendency to try too hard — to hurry, strain, press and try to blast the whole fight at once. As the athlete forces himself to give everything he has to the performance, his mental demands exceed his physical capacities. The result may be described as *generalized* rather than *specific effort*. Overall tension and unnecessary muscular contractions act as *brakes*, reducing speed and dissipating energy. The body performs better when the athlete *lets it go* than when he tries to drive it. When the athlete is running as fast as he can, he should not feel as though he ought to be running faster.

Elements that make greater speed possible:

Preliminary *warming up* to reduce viscosity, increase elasticity and flexibility, and tune the system to a higher physiological tempo (heart rate, blood flow and pressure, respiratory adjustment).

Preliminary *muscular tonus* and partial contraction.

A suitable *stance.*

Proper *attention focus.*

Reduction of stimuli-reception to *rapid perceptual habits* and reduction of the resultant movements to fast-reacting habit patterns.

After *momentum* in a throwing or elliptical striking movement has been generated by a long radius and a long arc in the swing, the speed may be increased without applying additional force by suddenly *shortening the radius of the arc.* This effect is seen in the "pull-in" at the last of the arc in the hammer throw, in the backward thrust against the forward leg by the batter in baseball, and so on. Snapping a towel or a whip are common examples of the same "shortened lever" principle.

The whiplike or coiled-spring action of the human body in its striking (throwing) movement-pattern is a remarkable phenomenon.

The whiplike or coiled-spring action of the human body in its striking (throwing) movement-pattern is a remarkable phenomenon. The movement of the body may start with a push of the toes, continue with a straightening of the knees and the trunk, add the shoulder rotation, the upper arm swing, and culminate in a forearm, wrist and finger snap. *The timing is such that each segment adds its speed to that of the others.* The shortened lever principle is used to accentuate many of the particular speeds of this uncoil or whip. The rotation of each segment around its particular joint-fulcrum is made at high speed for that particular part; but each segment rate is accelerated tremendously because it rotates around a fulcrum already highly accelerated.

In throwing a ball, all the accumulated speeds of the body are present at the elbow when the forearm snaps over its fast-moving elbow-fulcrum. Most of the distance-throwing or arched-striking acts illustrate these speed principles. One does not "hit with his feet" but he does start the momentum with his feet.

An important aspect of this multiple action of acceleration is the introduction of *each segment movement as late as possible* in order to take full advantage of the peak acceleration of its fulcrum. The arm is kept so far behind that the chest muscles pulling against it are tensed and stretched. The final wrist snap is postponed until the last instant before release or, in striking, before contact. In football, the punter puts the last snap into his knee and foot as, or a shade after, he makes contact with the ball. It is this *last moment acceleration* that is meant by "block through the man" in football or "*punch* through the man" in boxing. *The principle is to preserve the maximum acceleration up to the last instant of contact.* Regardless of distance, the final phase of a movement should be the *fastest.* Maintaining this increasing acceleration as long as there is contact is sound. This concept, however, is sometimes confused with the idea of a full, free, uninhibited motion of body inertia after the contact is over. This latter principle is sound only when such relaxed follow-through will not interfere with the speed of the next act.

Speed is a complex aspect. It includes *time of recognizing* and *time of reacting*. The more complex the situation to which one reacts, the slower one is likely to be. Thus, the effectiveness of feints.

The athlete can accelerate his speed by learning *proper awareness* (attention focus) and *suitable preparatory postures*. The rate at which he can contract his muscles is an important aspect in his relative speed.

Certain physical principles govern speed: shortened radius for quicker action, longer arc for imparting greater momentum, centering weight for speed in rotation and multiplying speed by sequential but concurrently overlapping movements. The question an individual athlete must answer is what kind of speed is most effective for his particular work method.

Often, it's not how fast it travels but how soon it gets there that counts.

Speed and timing are complementary and speed in delivering a stroke will lose most of its effectiveness unless the stroke is properly timed.

TIMING

Speed and timing are complementary and speed in delivering a stroke will lose most of its effectiveness unless the stroke is properly timed.

Reaction Time

Reaction time is the time gap between a stimulus and the response.

It may be more completely defined in two ways:

1. The time that elapses from the occurrence of the stimulus, or cue to act, to the *beginning* of the muscle movement.
2. The time from the occurrence of the stimulus to the *completion* of a simple muscular contraction.

Both definitions include the time taken for perception. If the perception is a simple thing like hearing a gun or seeing a flag dropped, the amount of possible improvement of perceptual speed is less. The techniques of *preparatory movement* can be improved so that response time is shortened. The direction of one's *attention (awareness)* to the motor act can shorten the response time. The remaining factor under the second definition is that of muscle contraction speed.

———————————

Total reaction consists of three elements:

1. The time required for the stimulus to reach the receivers (i.e.: audio, visual, tactile, etc.).
2. Plus the time required for the brain to relay the impulse through the proper nerve fibers to the proper muscles.
3. Plus the time required for the muscles to get into action after receiving the impulse.

———————————

Reaction time becomes longer under the following conditions:

The direction of one's attention (awareness) to the motor act can shorten the response time.

1. Not trained in any type of system
2. Tiredness
3. Absentmindedness
4. Emotionally upset (i.e.: anger, fear, etc.)

———————————

Opponent's reaction time is lengthened:

1. Immediately after the completion of a technique.
2. When his stimuli are combined.
3. When he is inhaling.
4. When he withdraws his energy (involves attitude).
5. When his attention or sight is misdirected.
6. Generally, when he is physically or mentally off-balance.

———————————

Warming up, physiological condition and degree of motivation, all affect general reaction time.

———————————

Movement Time

Movement time may be compared to fencing time. A period of fencing time *(temps d'escrime*) is the time taken by a fencer to perform one simple fencing movement. Such simple fencing action may be a single arm movement or a step forward.

The time taken to make a simple movement will vary according to the speed of the individual fighter.

Making an unexpected attack or the removal of the blade as the opponent is about to engage it are examples of actions executed *in time*.

It is not necessary to execute an action in time with a quick or violent motion. A movement that starts from rest without obvious preparation and proceeds *smoothly without hesitation* may be so unexpected that it succeeds in hitting the opponent before he is alerted.

Cause the opponent to lose a movement time:

1. By jamming him to disturb his rhythm.
2. By checking and controlling him (immobilization).
3. By drawing a preliminary reaction from him in the first half of your attack.
4. By deflecting his movement and scoring.

A good fighter must sense rather than perceive his chance to strike.

An action, although technically perfect, can be frustrated by the opponent's preventive hits. Therefore, it is absolutely essential to time the attack at exactly the right moment, psychologically or physically, when the opponent cannot avoid being hit.

Thus, timing means the ability to recognize the right moment and seize the opportunity for an action. Timing can be analyzed through its physical, physiological and psychological aspects.

A hit may be made as the opponent is preparing or planning to move.
A hit may land when the opponent is in the midst of a movement.
A hit may land in the fluctuating cyclic events of tension.
A hit may be made when the opponent is not paying attention, when his concentration flags.

This perfect moment may be either seized instinctively or provoked consciously. A good fighter must sense rather than perceive his chance to strike.

Timing Exercises:

1. Practice keeping the proper distance.
2. Attack when your partner changes position or is retracting his weapon.
3. Practice the *evasive thrust*, a simple attack in time against the opponent's attempt at engagement. The evasive thrust must be practiced against the simple, semi-circular and circular engagement.

Aim at quick hitting and do not sacrifice speed for power. A terrific kick and a powerful punch depend on two things: (a) leverage, (b) timing. Timing is an integral part of leverage, but the reverse is not the case. One does not need strength or weight to hit hard. *Timing a blow is the secret of powerful hitting.*

Timing one's blows in boxing means the art of hitting the rival *as he comes forward* or perhaps is lured into coming forward. The good fighter seems to out-guess his adversary and, whenever possible, takes the initiative and *influences the reaction* of his opponent. Then, his actions are carried out *purposefully and without hesitation. This requires confidence and no one — repeat, no one — can be a really heavy hitter through perfect timing unless he has* **complete** *faith in his own ability.*

Timing a blow is the secret of powerful hitting.

Broken Rhythm

Ordinarily, two fighters of equal ability can follow each other's movements and, unless there is a considerable difference in speed, they are very likely to stalemate each other. The movements of attacking and defending work almost in rhythm with each other. They have a sequential relationship which makes the proper timing of each movement dependent on the previous movement. Although there is a slight advantage in the initiative of the attack, it must also be backed by superior speed in order to land successfully. However, when the rhythm is broken, speed is no longer the primary element in the success of the attack or counterattack of the man who has broken the rhythm. If the rhythm has been well established, there is a tendency to continue in the sequence of the movement. In other words, each man is "*motorset*" to continue the sequence. The man who can break this rhythm by a light hesitation or an unexpected movement can now score an attack or counterattack with only moderate speed; his opponent is motorset to continue with the previous rhythm and before he can adjust himself to the change, he has been hit. That is why the stroke on time is usually a pretty stroke, for it seems to catch its victim flatfooted.

Timing has to be felt and mastered as a psychological problem, even more than as a fighting problem, for the breaking of the rhythm relies on the fact that *the victim is going to continue for a fraction of a second in the sequence of movements which has suddenly been interrupted.*

Sometimes, timing involves attacking with many threatening movement (feints). *If the defender accepts this rhythm* and attempts to parry these various threats, then a slight hesitation will break the rhythm and provide the opportune moment to launch the final attack. On other occasions, when your opponent is in the midst of making advances or threatening movements on his own account, you may succeed in breaking the rhythm by first apparently reacting as he expects and then suddenly launching a counterattack when he thinks you should be following his feint. You should land, for he is motorset to continue with his threats and cannot adjust himself to the necessity of parrying until after you have scored. In general, timing here means that you initiate your attack or movement when your opponent has started preparation of an attack. Thus, timing becomes a question of taking advantage of the slight interval before he can readjust himself to make a parry.

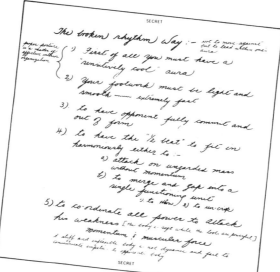

One-and-a-half beat

A correctly judged cadence permits the calm control of every stroke.

Any attack performed halfway through the opponent's movement is said to occur on the half-beat. When the fighter lulls his opponent's rhythm by inducing or performing one full-count movement, he may then "break the trance" by striking on the half-beat. This broken rhythm method will often catch the opponent mentally and physically off balance for defense.

Cadence

Speed, *regulated to coincide with the adversary's*, is known as *"cadence."* It is the *specific* rhythm at which a succession of movements is executed.

A correctly judged cadence permits the calm control of every stroke. This control will allow the fighter to select, with more ease, the movements of offense and defense which will bring about a hit.

Remember that to land a hit, *the defense has to be avoided.* Excessive speed can catch up with the opponent's parries. The attacker is then known as "having parried himself."

Ideally, a fighter *should seek to* impose his cadence on an opponent. This may be achieved by *intentionally varying the cadence of his own movements.* For example, he can deliberately establish a certain rhythm in his feints in a composite attack until the defender is induced to follow that cadence.

By obtaining an edge of speed on the adversary, the fighter may lead him. In other words, it is the adversary who continually will have to try to catch up. If one has a sufficient margin of speed on hand, it is possible to maintain this advantage. To do so must have a moral effect on the opponent who, finding himself subjected to his adversary's will in this important factor of speed, cannot fail to suffer in his confidence.

The preparation by a series of false attacks and feints, executed at a normal rhythm, has the effect of lulling the opponent into a false sense of preparedness. It accustoms his reactions to a cadence other than that which will be used for the attack itself. Then, the movements comprising the final attack are *suddenly accelerated* and more likely to find him lagging behind.

That little fragment of time (one beat in a cadence) which is the most suitable to accomplish effective action is called "tempo."

A very effective change of cadence is to *slow down*, instead of speed up, the final action of a compound attack or riposte. This slowing of cadence can be pictured as a strike whose delivery is begun, halted in its path forward and continued when the adversary leaves the threatened line for another in the hope of finding the hand.

Speed, applied *at the opportune moment*, together with the correctly judged cadence in the execution of the movement, will go a long way toward ensuring the success of a stroke.

Tempo

The success of a movement, defensive or offensive, depends on whether we perform it at the right time or not. We must *surprise* our opponent and catch the moment of his *helplessness*.

That *little fragment of time* (one beat in a cadence) which is the most suitable to accomplish effective action is called *"tempo."*

From a *psychological point of view*, the moment of surprise and, from the *physical point of view*, the moment of helplessness are the right moments to attack. This is the true conception of tempo — *choosing the exact psychological and physical moment of weakness in an opponent.*

There are also tempo opportunities when the opponent makes conscious movement, that is, when he steps forward, makes an invitation, goes into a bind, etc. In such and similar cases, the moment for attack is *when he is executing the movement* because *until he finishes it, he cannot change to the reverse.*

Every action at the peak of the art of fighting is *tempo,* but be careful that the adversary does not mislead you by giving false tempo opportunities.

Attack when your opponent is *preoccupied,* when he is preparing *his* offensive, on his advance, his absence of touch, his engagement and change of same. Such requires an unceasing concentration and vigilance.

Regard your opponent's concentration in terms of a graph and *attack in the depressions,* in *his moments of irresolution.*

The choice of time is the supreme factor in the success of an offensive. Develop it. Even faultless technique and lightning rapidity will fail if the attack is launched "out of time."

The "how to" is important but to be successful necessitates the "why" and the "when."

We must surprise our opponent and catch the moment of his helplessness.

Stop-hit

When the distance is wide, the attacking opponent requires some sort of preparation. Therefore, attack him on his preparation of attack.

A stop-hit is a timed hit made against the adversary at the same time he is making an attack. It *anticipates and intercepts* the final line of attack and is delivered in such a way that the executant is covered, either by being in line behind the hit or by supplementary covering. To ensure success, it must have correct anticipation and timing, plus precise placement.

Essentially, a stop-hit arrests the opponent in the development of his attack. It can be direct or indirect. It may be used as he steps forward to kick or punch, when he is preoccupied with feinting, or between two moves of a complicated combination.

Stop-hit

1. On the opponent's preparation of stepping forward.
2. To stop his attack while his arm is still bent.
3. When the opponent feints very wide, exposing his guard.
4. Against an attack with wide, badly directed hand movements.
5. Before applying immobilization (using a direct or indirect stop-hit).
6. On the first feint from the on-guard position before lunging with a real attack.

The stop-hit is an excellent means of defense against an opponent (especially against his advanced parts and exposed lines) who attacks wildly with insufficient care to covering or against one who just comes too close.

Correct appreciation of *time* and *distance* is essential to making an effective stop-hit. While it is usually made with a straight thrust or kick, the stop-hit may also be part of a disengagement or counter-disengagement, or may be done while ducking or slipping.

Sometimes the stop-hit necessitates some angulation of the body in order to dominate the opponent's hand.

We can therefore say that generally the stop-hit is the stroke chosen to deal with the *stepping preparation*.

The stop-hit oftentimes necessitates a step forward to land ahead of the opponent's focus. It is advisable, at least, to lean forward as if to meet the attacker.

A stop-hit is more often useful and successful against attacks that begin with a step forward, where the margin of time allowing for success is greater than against attacks not preceded by a step. We can therefore say that generally the stop-hit is the stroke chosen to deal with the *stepping preparation*.

A person should train himself to be constantly prepared to make a stop-hit during the course of any movement of a phase. The successful introduction of a stop-hit not only enables many valuable hits to be scored, but has a devastating moral effect on a forceful and confident opponent. Train to stop-hit with great *speed* and *accuracy* from a *variety of angles*.

Counter-time

It is not wise at all to attack without first having gained control of the opponent's movement time or hand position. Thus, a smart fighter uses every means at his disposal, patiently and systematically, to draw the stop-hit. It brings the adversary's hand or leg within his reach and gives him the opportunity to gain control of it.

The second-intention attack or "*counter-time*" is a *premeditated* movement generally used against a fighter who has formed the habit of continually attempting stop-hits or who attacks into the attack; that is to say, one who launches an attack as soon as his opponent makes any offensive moment.

Counter-time is the strategy by which an opponent is induced or provoked to attack *in tempo*, with the object of counter-timing or alternatively taking possession of the opposing hand or detaching it and executing a subsequent attack or riposte. It lies not so much in drawing the stop-hit as in correctly timing the parry which deflects it. The speed of the opponent's reactions will have to be found and his cadence judged.

Distance must be judged correctly to minimize the danger of being hit while within reach of the opponent in order to land the final movement of the counter-time sequence (the riposte).

It is not wise at all to attack without first having gained control of the opponent's movement time or hand position.

The success of a counter-time movement largely depends on concealing one's real intentions and inducing the opponent to make his stop-hit with conviction, so that he has little opportunity to recover when it is parried before the riposte lands.

The stop-hit may be drawn in a variety of ways:

    #   By use of invitation (simply exposing targets)
    #   By intentionally uncovered feints
    #   By making false attacks with a half-lunge or merely by stepping forward.

It might be wise to riposte with opposition by immobilizing the opponent's stop-hit or alternate weapons, or by attacking in an evasive manner (i.e.: From varying body positions or using other than direct attacks).

Watch out for his purposely launching a stop-hit as a feint or he will parry the riposte and score with a counter-riposte. (He might induce one to use counter-time by showing an apparent predilection for stop-hitting.)

Attacks and ripostes, however well-designed and executed, will generally fail unless they are delivered at the right moment (timing) and at the right speed (cadence). A simple example of the right choice of time is provided by an attack by disengagement. From the normal on-guard position, a disengagement can be parried by a lateral movement of the hand which travels a matter of a few inches, while the attacker's hand has to travel several feet to reach the target. Under these conditions, the fastest attack should be parried by an even, slow defensive movement. This disparity in time will be aggravated if the attack is directed on a side of the target toward which the defender's hand is already moving to close the line.

It is obvious that the attack should be timed to move toward a part of the target from which the opponent's hand is moving, that is, *into an opening rather than a closing line*, if it is to have the best chance of overcoming the disadvantage of time and distance to which it is always subject.

Similarly, an excellent moment to launch an attack is *when the opponent is preparing an attack*. His intention and hand movements will then be momentarily concentrated more on attack than defense.

An excellent moment to launch an attack is *when the opponent is preparing an attack*.

An attack on preparation is often effective against an opponent who maintains a particularly accurate distance measure and who is difficult to reach because he keeps just out of attacking distance whenever an offensive movement is made. The attack can be made after the opponent has been drawn within distance and induced to prepare an attack by a short step back.

An attack on preparation must not be confused with an attack into an attack. The former is made during the preparation and *before* the opponent's attack begins, while the attack into an attack is, in fact, a counter-offensive movement. A very exact choice of distance and careful timing is required if the attack on preparation is to obtain priority in time over the opponent's attack.

ATTITUDE

The state of the athlete's mind as he faces his event determines the degree of excess tension he will carry into the event. The athlete free from excess tension as he awaits his performance is typically self-confident. He has what is commonly known as "*a winning attitude*." He sees himself as master of the athletic situation confronting him. To many athletes, being a champion is a matter of "psychological necessity." Fed by previous successes and having completely rationalized previous failure, he feels himself a Triton among minnows.

As an event approaches, the athlete often notices a feeling of weakness in his midsection (butterflies in his stomach), feels nauseated and may vomit; his heart pounds, he may experience pain in his lower back. The experienced athlete recognizes these sensations *not as an inner weakness*, but as *an inner surplus*. These signs indicate a *preparedness for violent activity*. In fact, the athlete who expresses a feeling of euphoria before an event is probably in a poor state of readiness. Many athletes call it *"adrenalburger,"* a conditon affected by adrenomedullary activity, augmented by the stimulating effect of the competitive situation.

If emotional control is not well-learned, critical moments in the fight when the emotional tension is highest will result in loss of skill by the fighter. His muscles suddenly must work against his own over-tense antagonistic muscles. He becomes stiff and clumsy in his movements. Expose yourself to various conditions and learn.

Experience shows that an athlete who forces himself to the limit can keep going as long as necessary. This means that ordinary effort will not tap or release the tremendous store of reserve power latent in the human body. Extraordinary effort, highly emotionalized conditions or a true determination to win at all costs will release this extra energy. Therefore, an athlete is actually as tired as he feels and, if he is determined to win, he can keep on almost indefinitely to achieve his objective. The attitude, "You can win if you want to badly enough," means that the will to win is constant. No amount of punishment, no amount of effort, no condition is too "tough" to take in order to win. Such an attitude can be developed only if winning is closely tied to the practitioner's ideals and dreams.

The real competitor is the one who gives all he has, all the time.

A practitioner must learn to perform at top speed all the time, not to coast with the idea that he can "open up" when the time comes. The real competitor is the one who gives all he has, all the time. The result is that he works close to his capacity at all times and in so doing, forms an *attitude* of giving all he has. In order to create such an attitude, the practitioner must be driven longer, harder and faster than normally would be required.

Use attitude to create:

1. Evasiveness with very light movement (but not passive!!)
2. Devastating attacks
3. Speed
4. Natural dynamics
5. Deception and slipperiness
6. Stickiness and directness
7. Complete ease

TOOLS

Before I studied the art, a punch to me was just a punch, a kick was just a kick. After I'd studied the art, a punch was no longer a punch, a kick no longer a kick. Now that I understand the art, a punch is just a punch, a kick is just a kick.

Western boxing is too over-daring because of restrictions on illegal and "unfair" tactics as compared to the over-protectiveness of the Oriental martial arts caused by the no-hold -barred, full bodily target. In addition, the no-contact practice of stopping the attacks several inches in front of the target in the Oriental martial arts creates a habitual false sense of distance. From this dust waving act in front of a moving target rather than the timed explosion through a moving target springs negligence in the practice of evasive tactics. The evasive tactics are so much a part of an aggressive art such as boxing. Slips, ducks, weaves are all a sort of aggressive defense without moving the body out of range.

In realistic, total fighting, we must embody the practical elements of both of the above tactics. We must use range as a protective device as well as use the evasive tactics of in-fighting. Neither by itself is reliable enough for success in total fighting.

Evasive tactics combined with punishment can be applied in no-hold-barred fighting during the opponent's final extended commitment and during the gaps between two progressive exertions toward you. These tactics will serve to take the play away from an aggressor or will initiate grappling.

In boxing, it is a correct maxim that a good offense is the best defense. A good offense consists of *leads, false moves* and *counterpunches supported by mobility, pressure* and *generalship.*

> It is a correct maxim that a good offense is the best defense.

A good boxer is able to beat his opponent to the punch with lightning fast leads and draw out his opponent's counterpunches with feints in such a way as to make the counterpunches miss. The opponent's miss leaves him out of position and an easy target for a counterpunch from the boxer doing the leading.

It is the ability to outsmart an opponent and out-maneuver him that is the skill and science of the sport of boxing. To have this ability, you must understand hitting (and kicking) and the different types of blows (and kicks) there are, and when and where each type is best put to use. You must develop combinations of punches (and/or kicks) that work well. As the result of long practice, you must become able to put your full weight and strength into your punch (and kick). You must deliver the right blow at the proper time, automatically.

When you have developed hitting (and kicking) into something automatic, it will become instantaneous and your mind will be free to plan your battle as the fight progresses and new situations arise. You can only reach this point of development if you have been

willing to do the necessary training. That training grind is the most valuable thing boxing has to offer.

The elements of attack are all used to carry the attack through strategy, requiring speed, deception, timing and judgment. They are the tools of the master craftsman who blends them into perfect attacks.

Attack by deception, especially, is the attack of the master. The master boxer has at his command techniques that bewilder and confuse the opponent, thereby creating many openings. He feints his opponent into "knots." He combines hitting with feints in such a manner that both appear to be the same. He draws his opponent to him, *forcing whatever he desires.* Through defensive hitting and judicious movement, he *keeps his opponent off-balance.* The master boxer has the ability to get in close and understands the value of in-fighting. He has so perfected the *shift* that it is used for attack as well as defense. Finally, he is the master of counter-fighting, for he knows *when to attack* and *when to allow attack.* Scientific attack, then, is no simple matter, but requires years of study and practice for its successful use.

Attack by deception, especially, is the attack of the master.

In the process of attack, there are four basic methods that you will use often: leading, feinting, drawing and in-fighting.

Leading

The master of attack must know the value of a *straight lead.* He must know what is liable to happen on any lead. He realizes that for every lead, there is an opening and for every opening, a counter and for every counter, a parry or a counter-time. These things he understands, but he also knows *how* and *when* to lead with comparative safety.

Leading with the forward hand, guarding with the rear hand, while moving to the side, makes negligible any opening that ordinarily results from a straight forward lead with the hand.

Feinting

Feinting is characteristic of the expert fighter. It requires using the eyes, the hands, the body and the legs in a single effort to deceive an opponent. These movements are really decoys and if the opponent attempts to adjust his defense, the expert takes advantage of the openings created. Feinting is also used to ascertain what the opponent's reaction will be to each movement.

Feinting creates only momentary openings. To be able to take advantage of these openings means instant reflex action or foreknowledge of what openings will be created by certain feints. Such familiarity is presupposed by practice, for only through the actual practicing of many feints against many kinds of opponents may a general reaction tendency be determined. If an opening is created by a certain feint, that opening should not be used until a clean, sure blow will result. A good fighter knows what openings will result before he feints and makes use of his knowledge by initiating his follow-up action almost before the opening results. Whenever two fighters of equal speed, strength and skill are matched, the one who is the master of the feint will be the winner.

The essential elements in feinting are *rapidity*, *change*, *deception* and *precision*, followed by clean crisp blows. Feints used too often in the same way will enable the opponent to time them for a counterattack, thus defeating their very purpose.

Feints against the unskilled are not as necessary as against the skilled. Many different combinations of feints should be practiced until they are natural movements.

Drawing

Drawing is closely allied to feinting. Whereas in feinting an opening is created, in drawing some part of the body is left unprotected in order that a particular blow will be led by the opponent, thus developing the opportunity to use a specific counter.

Whenever two fighters of equal speed, strength and skill are matched, the one who is the master of the feint will be the winner.

Feinting is only a part of drawing. *Drawing uses the method of strategy and the method of crowding or forcing.* Being able to advance while apparently open to attack, but ready to counter if successful, is a phase of fighting that few ever develop. Many fighters refuse to lead. Then, to be able to draw or force a lead becomes very important.

In-fighting

This is the art of fighting at close range. Not only does it take skill to get in close, but it takes skill to stay there. To get inside, it is necessary to slip, bob and weave, draw and feint.

Because of the many variables, fighting is a careful game. It should be readily understood that each hit must be painstakingly and patiently prepared. Yet, it is generally fatal to start a bout with a set plan. Stay actively aware, but ever flexible.

You must deliver
the right blow at
the proper time,
automatically.

SOME WEAPONS FROM JKD

LEG TECHNIQUES

A. SIDE KICK (Primarily lead leg)
1. Downward side kick
   (shin/knee and thigh)
2. Parallel side kick
   (ribs, stomach, kidneys, etc.)
3. Upward side kick
4. Angle-in high side kick
   (right lead to left stance
   and vice versa)
5. Angle-in low side kick
6. Slide-in drop side kick
   (upward or parallel thrust)
7. Step-back shin/knee side kick
   (counter)
8. Leaping side kick
9. Reverse shin/knee stop-kick
   (with arch of rear foot)

B. LEADING STRAIGHT KICK
1. Toe kick
   (lead and counter to groin)
2. High straight kick
3. Medium straight kick
4. Low straight kick
5. Angle-in straight kick
6. Rising straight kick
   (to knee or wrist)
7. Step-back straight kick
8. Leaping straight kick
9. Downward front cross stomp

C. REVERSE STRAIGHT KICK
1. High reverse straight kick
2. Medium reverse straight kick
3. Low reverse straight kick
4. Angle-in reverse straight kick
   (high, medium, low)
5. Step-back reverse straight kick
6. Reverse cross stomp

D. HOOK KICK
1. Leading hook (high, medium, low)
2. Reverse hook (high, medium, low)
3. Leading one-two hook

4. Reverse one-two hook
5. Double leaping hook
6. Step-back hook
7. Vertical hook
8. Inverted hook

E. SPIN BACK KICK
1. High spin back kick
2. Medium spin back kick
3. Low spin back kick
4. Step-back spin back kick (counter)
5. Leaping spin back kick
6. Vertical spin back kick
7. Spin back wheel kick (360°)

F. HOOKING HEEL KICK
(stiff-legged or bent)
1. High hooking heel kick
2. Medium hooking heel kick
3. Low hooking heel kick
4. Leading one-two hooking heel kick
5. Reverse one-two hooking heel kick
   (with rear foot)

G. KNEE THRUST
1. Leading upward knee thrust
2. Leading inward knee thrust
3. Reverse upward knee thrust
   (rear knee)
4. Reverse inward knee thrust
   (rear knee)

HAND TECHNIQUES

A. LEADING FINGER JAB
1. Long-range finger jab
   (high, medium, low)
2. Close-range finger jab
   —the poke
3. Corkscrew finger fan

*B. STRAIGHT LEADING
PUNCH AND JAB*
1. High straight lead
2. Medium straight lead (to body)
3. Low straight lead
4. Slanting right

5. Slanting left

6. Double straight lead

C. LEADING HOOK

1. High lead hook

2. Medium lead hook

3. Low lead hook

4. Tight

5. Loose

6. Upward (shovel)

7. Horizontal

8. Forward and downward
   (corkscrew)

9. Palm hook

D. REAR CROSS

1. High rear cross

2. Medium rear cross

3. Low rear cross

4. Overhand downward stroke
   (corkscrew hook or palm)

5. Upward groin strike

E. BACKFIST

1. High backfist

2. Medium backfist

3. Low backfist

4. Vertical backfist
   (upward, downward)

5. Stiff-armed
   (big backfist)

F. QUARTER SWING (shortened arc)

1. With palm

2. With back of fist

3. Reverse quarter swing (rear hand)

4. With finger fan

G. UPPERCUT

1. High uppercut

2. Medium uppercut

3. Low uppercut (bolo to groin)

4. Reverse ridge hand to groin

H. REVERSE SPIN BLOW

1. With bottomfist

2. With forearm

3. With elbow

4. Double spinning blow

I. HAMMER BLOW

1. Left hammer

2. Right hammer

3. Downward hammer

ELBOW TECHNIQUES

1. Upward elbow

2. Downward elbow

3. Twisting downward

4. Backward elbow

5. Smashing right

6. Smashing left

HEAD BUTT

1. Lunging forward

2. Lunging backward

3. Lunging right

4. Lunging left

ETC.

GRAPPLING

1. Wrestling: Strangulation (hair control)
              Leg tackles
              Tie-ups

2. Judo: Joint locks
         Chokes
         Leverage timing

MENTAL CULTIVATION

1. Krishnamurti

2. Zen

3. Taoism

CONDITIONING

1. General: Running
             Flexibility

2. Specialized: Boxing
                Kicking
                Wrestling

3. Strength: Weights
             Special apparatus

NUTRITION

1. Break down/build up

2. Muscular diet

It is the ability to outsmart an opponent and out-maneuver him that is the skill and science of the sport of boxing.

KICKING

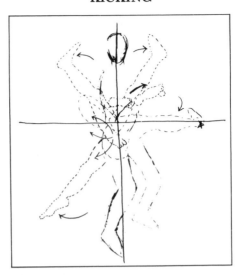

What are the Choices of Target in terms of easiness, safety, efficiency?

Choices of Target in terms of easiness, safety and efficiency

a) hook: (1) R-stancer's frontal knee
   (2) R-stancer's groin
   (3) R-stancer's head
   (4) L-stancer's knee
   (5) L-stancer's head

[Note: investigate body feel to inflict force on unfamiliar but direct target areas on R and L-stancer. Remember L-rear hook.]

b) side: (1) R-stancer's shin/knee
   (2) L-stancer's shin/knee

[Note: Close-range downward thrust (instep, shin, knee) — also cross stomp.]

c) reverse hook: (1) L-stancer's frontal knee
   (2) R-stancer's knee

d) lead forward thrust: look into knee, groin

e) L-(rear) forward thrust

f) L-spin kick

g) vertical hook kick

h) R-finger jab — 3 ways

i) R-jab — (3 ways and high/low)

j) R-hook — high/low

k) R-back fist — high/low

l) left cross — high/low

m) right bottom fist (forward hand)

n) L (rear) bottom fist — (reverse, spin)

o) possible combinations of kicks
   (1) natural follow-up
   (2) trained follow-up

p) possible combinations of hands

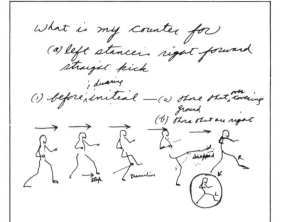

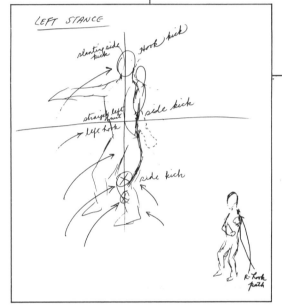

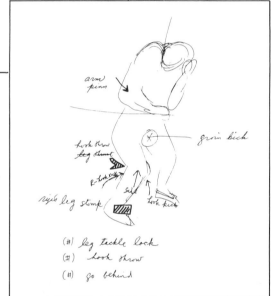

A good offense consists of leads, false moves and counterpunches supported by mobility, pressure and generalship.

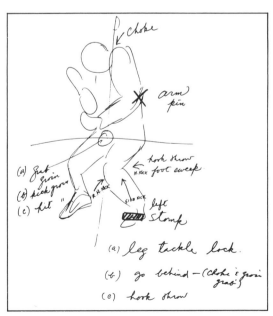

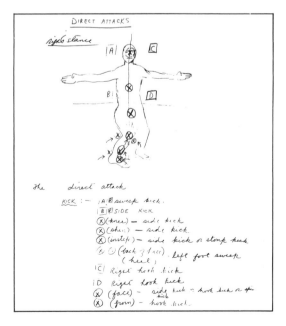

Savate's Purring Kick — (circular or upward force)

a) Knee does not have mobility like upper body.

b) Thrown to the front and rear.

c) Quickest (economic), most powerful (natural) and hardest to move away from.

d) Heel normally makes contact. Experiment making contact with the ball of the foot.

e) Sometimes it is necessary to bypass the front to attack the rear weight-bearing leg. The more weight on the leg, the more damage to the knee.

In realistic, total fighting, we must embody the practical elements of evasion and aggression.

Kicking technique must:

1) have a sense of powerful ease, developed through practice and supplementary exercises.

2)   be able to adjust height in initiation.

3)   be economically sudden in initiation.

4)   have smooth speed.

5)   be able to blend with any movement.

6)   be direct and instantaneous in relaying tool part to target area.

7)   be accurate and precise.

Functions of the longest kicks —

1)   Primarily to reach a more distant target

2)   As a destructing tool

3)   To bridge the gap for another kick or hand technique

The kick you use will vary according to the type of opponent you face.

The attacking lunge (step and slide and all the attacking steps) must:

1)   facilitate a speedy recovery out of range of a counterkick, should the attack fail. The slightest loss of balance or control may mean that some part of a counterkick target has been left unprotected for a fraction of a second.

2)   be able to overcome the long measure with speed, economy and control.

3)   have an element of surprise, catching the opponent off guard mentally or physically.

4)   be driven with great determination and speed/power once initiated.

5)   use maximum reach to kick the target (3/4 bend or more, especially in attack). That extended distance is what makes an all kicking attack possible.

6)   utilize intense grace and awareness, comparable to the hand, and explode with killing power — that's the art of kicking.

Western boxing is too over-daring because of restrictions on illegal and "unfair" tactics.

Develop power on the spot —

   a)   During combinations with the same leg.

        —   high/low hook and shin/knee side

        —   high/low and angle-in hook kick

   b)   During alternate leg kicking.

   c)   During reaching, extended reaching, hooking.

   d)   During close-range thrusting.

        —   Apply close-range side kick downward to avoid jamming and to add a powerful tool.

        —   Consider kneeing in close-range and stomping while maintaining balanced posture.

Develop "body feel" (distance, timing, releasing, etc.) of tossing your tool part at a moving target while moving yourself. Learn to *relay* your weapon part while you are in motion.

a) Heel — straight, side, cross
b) Ball — upward, straight, sides
c) Toe
d) Instep
e) Both sides — sideswipe motions of hooking, reaping, sweeping

---

Combine kicking with all phases of footwork.
a) Advance, all types
b) Retreat, all types
c) Circling left, all types
d) Circling right, all types
e) Parallel moving

Notes on the speed kick — Like a cobra, the fast kick should be felt and not seen.

Use the speedy delivery of kicks to "arrest" your opponent's "moving away from neutrality."

Use the speedy delivery of kicks to "jump" your opponent's consciousness. Find an attitude of loosening antagonistic muscles prior to delivery, a "continuous waiting" attitude rather than a "preparatory" one. Use the speedy delivery of kicks to "arrest" your opponent's "moving away from neutrality."

"Watch" the delivery, landing and recovery *with continuous awareness*, reinforcing all with "watchful" hand guards.

Balancing center —

Initiation:
a) looseness in neutrality
b) economical start that blends with neutrality
c) playful looseness (mental)
   and smooth speed (physical)

Transition:
a) clear sight
b) neutrality
c) regulated balance
d) tight defense

Landing:
- a)   well-timed collision with right part of tool
- b)   natural releasing of coordinated destructive force

―――――――――――   ‑‑‑   ―――――――――――

Recovery:
- a)   flowing back to neutrality or flow on with attack
- b)   reinforcement with "watchfulness"

―――――――――――   ‑‑‑   ―――――――――――

Which are the safety "speed" lead kicks used as pace setters, respect getters, distance gougers? How much faster can you make them without turning them into "flickiness?" Note: Use the boxing jab as a guideline. For instance, you wouldn't use the rear hook unless you are pretty certain of securing distance and opponent's condition. Learn how *not* to let the opponent take advantage of your commitment. Psyche your opponent, physically and mentally, by inflicting pain.

―――――――――――   ‑‑‑   ―――――――――――

List kicks that snap from the knee such as:
>   groin hook kick (inward snap)
>   reverse hook (outward snap)
>   upward snap kick
>   straight forward snap kick

Psyche your opponent, physically and mentally, by inflicting pain.

―――――――――――   ‑‑‑   ―――――――――――

List kicks that thrust from the hips such as:
>   side thrust kick
>   back thrust kick
>   front thrust kick

―――――――――――   ‑‑‑   ―――――――――――

Look into snapping a kick from the knee to get more power, or snapping a kick from the hip and knee to get more speed. Test both in long, medium (natural firing distance) and close range.

―――――――――――   ‑‑‑   ―――――――――――

What are the pacing kicks that are snappy and combine with quick retreat?
Note: They should slow the pursuer by hitting into his line of movement while you are moving off his line of force.

―――――――――――   ‑‑‑   ―――――――――――

What are the pacing kicks that jam?
Note: Work out precautions for being grabbed.

What are the close-range kicks that thrust and that snap?
Note: Work out natural hand or leg follow-ups.

Possible Angle Positions of Front Leg:

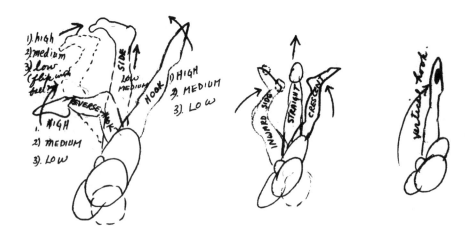

Note: Learn "relaying destructive force" to "where" the target is or is headed. Use "body feel" as your guideline.

Learn "relaying destructive force" to "where" the target is or is headed.

Possible Angle Positions of Rear Leg:

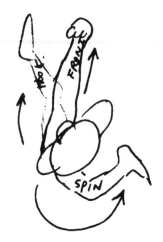

What are the strongest kicks in terms of destructive power?
What are those that can most easily score on the opponent?

KICKING METHODS
   — Upward
   — Downward
   — Outside in
   — Inside out
   — Straight on

Examples with front leg kicks:

Instep Upward Groin Kick — (upward force)

(close-range/medium-range)

Note: Experiment on body feel to relay the most destruction to opponent's:

(1) shin

(2) knee

(3) groin

(4) ?

Vertical Hook — (upward force)

(medium range)

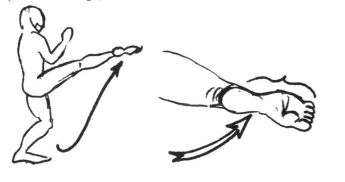

Use "body feel" as your guideline.

Hook Kick — (outside in)

Watch leaning for balance and recovery.

High — Medium — Low

Long — Medium — Close Range

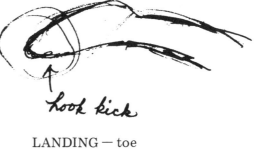

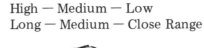

LANDING — toe

               instep

               ball

               shin

               inside foot swipe

Learn what muscles are involved in this kick and how to limber the parts.

———————

Important: Relax timing muscles but keep an overall alertness of position and timing.

———————

Look into using the ball of the foot for attacking the shin, knee or instep.

———————

Reverse Hook Kick — (inside out)

Side Kick — (straight on, upward, downward, inside angle)

Range: long

medium

close (downward stomp)

In combat: The side kick is best utilized by directing it downward.

Develop in the side kick a sense of "delicate ease."

Learn the most efficient bridging of distance, plus efficient timing with the opponent's movement.

SHIN/KNEE KICKS
Methods:
— Straight on
— Straight down
— Inside out (such as reverse hook kick)
— Outside in (such as hook kick)

Decide which shin/knee kicks are progressively longer:
— shin/knee side
— shin/knee hook
— shin/knee reverse hook
— straight on shin/knee (front and rear)

———————

All should be done with speed and sudden economy in mind, as well as with power. Learn the most efficient bridging of distance, plus efficient timing with the opponent's movement.

The Leading Shin/Knee Side Kick

This kick can be an explosive, crispy thrust or a pushing thrust to wrench the opponent's knee while bridging the gap for a leg or hand follow-up. It has a very demoralizing effect and causes the opponent to attack less confidently. It also imposes respect of distance.

As an attack — to a right stancer

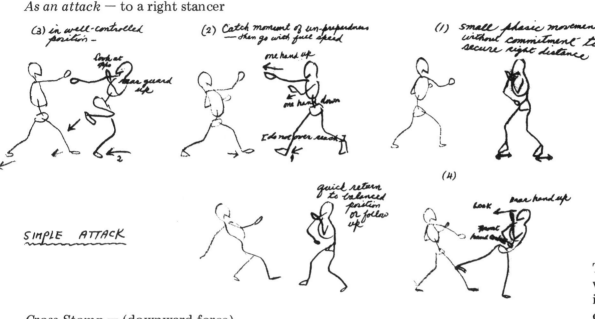

SIMPLE ATTACK

The kick has a very demoralizing effect and causes the opponent to attack less confidently.

Cross Stomp — (downward force)

Front Leg: Rear Leg:

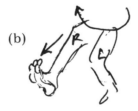

(a)   (b)

(hip closing)   (hip opening)

Name kicks that can be initiated without changing on-guard positioning before and/or after, such as: hook kick, side kick, vertical hook and reverse hook.

Front leg path without changing on-guard position too much.

Rear leg path without changing on-guard position too much.

(Note: The straight ⋀ has many slight variations of path.)

Of these economy kicks, which, besides the hook kick, go for absolute speed?

———————————— ·-·- ————————————

Guard from flickiness — find a happy medium, however, with speed in mind. Work on that particular *initiation economy* and not just on those kicks with non-changing, on-guard movements. Instead, have that *sudden economy* be the guideline at the drop of a dime.

———————————— ·-·- ————————————

Powerful Kicks With Non-Commitment

    Note: Use speedy delivery.

Hook Kick Example

Have that sudden economy be the guideline at the drop of a dime.

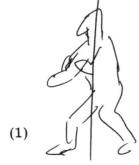

(1)

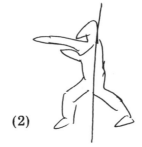

(2)

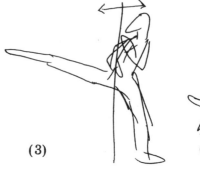

(3)

(4)

Small Phasic Bent Knee Position (neutral)

Economic Initiation

Find the point for quick recovery to neutrality. (This concerns all kicks.)

The Basic Kick Insertion (without footwork)

(1)

(2)

Front Leg

(shift forward)

Rear Leg

Learn how to cover initiation and the quick recovery to neutrality. Covering should be automatic and continual.

———————————— ·-·- ————————————

Name kicks that involve the absolute changing of on-guard positioning before and/or after initiation.

———————————— ·-·- ————————————

Study the leverage in still initiation.

Master kicking quickly and powerfully from high, low or ground posture. Develop body feel and efficient form in dropping suddenly to fast, powerful kicks while advancing, retreating, circling left, circling right. Learn to use "energy flow" to rise from unaccustomed squatting positions.

Upright —
frontal, sideways, circling

Crouch to Ground —
frontal, sideways, circling away

Air —
frontal, sideways, circling

You must develop combinations of punches (and/or kicks) that work well.

Develop the ability to apply a sweep with the economy of a kick. Look into initiating

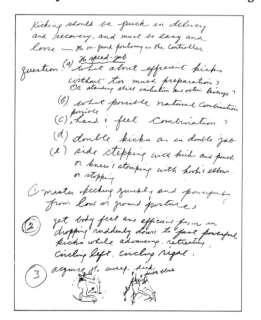

the foot sweep, with or without hand work, as a counter or attack at long, medium and close range.

Practice foot sweep and take down: (a) from a fast initiation, (b) as part of a combination and (c) as a counterattack.

study body-feel to get speed, fluidity & power.

(a)

(b) 掃腔腿

(c) *reverse leg sickle using heel.*

Note :— learn to put "energy flow" to rise from unaccustomed squatting postures.

Study kicking while a man is down:

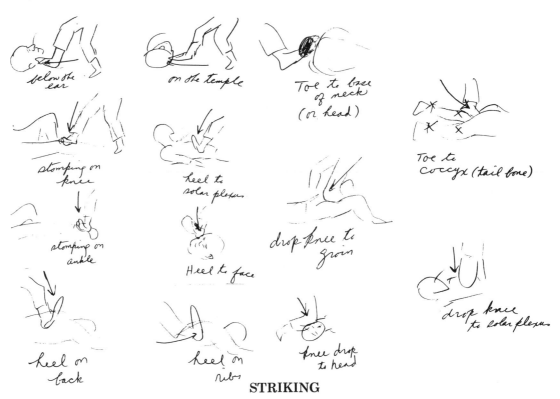

The leading straight punch is the backbone of all punching in Jeet Kune Do.

below the ear

on the temple

Toe to base of neck (or head)

Toe to coccyx (tail bone)

stomping on knee

heel to solar plexus

drop knee to groin

stomping on ankle

Heel to face

drop knee to solar plexus

heel on back

heel on ribs

knee drop to head

STRIKING

LEADING STRAIGHT PUNCH

The leading straight punch is the backbone of all punching in Jeet Kune Do. It is used both as an offensive and defensive weapon to "stop" and "intercept" an opponent's complex attack at a moment's notice. When you are standing right foot forward, your right punch and right leg become the main offensive weapons because of their advanced position. With your right foot forward, your right hand is much closer to your opponent than your left. The reverse is true for the left foot forward stance. When fighting, keep your strongest side up front.

The leading straight punch is the fastest of all punches. With the minimum movements involved in delivery, balance is not disturbed and, because it goes straight toward the

target, it has a better chance of landing. (The opponent has less time to block.) Also, the straight punch is more accurate than other punches.

No one punch, not even the efficient straight lead, can be an end in itself, though there are styles that use nothing but straight line punching. The straight lead is used as a means to an end and definitely should be reinforced and supported by other angle punches (and kicks), making your weapons more flexible without confinement to any one line. After all, a good man should be able to strike from all angles and with either hand (or leg) to take advantage of the moment.

The delivery of the straight punch is different from the traditional classical gung fu. First of all, the punch is never positioned on the hip, nor does it start from there. This way of delivery is unrealistic and exposes too great an area to protect. Of course, this also adds unnecessary distance to travel toward the opponent.

In Jeet Kune Do, you never strike your opponent with your fist only; you strike him with your whole body. In other words, you should not hit with just arm power; the arms are there as a means to transmit great force with the correct timing of feet, waist, shoulder and wrist motion at great speed.

The important point is not to have any classical "get-set" posture or preparatory movements prior to delivering the straight punch — or any punch for that matter.

Instead of coming from the shoulder, the punch is thrown from the center of the body in the form of a vertical fist, thumb up, and straight toward the front of your own nose. The nose here is the center guiding line. The wrist is slightly turned *downward* before delivery and is immediately *straightened upon impact* to add a corkscrew effect to the opponent.

The important point is not to have any classical "get-set" posture or preparatory movements prior to delivering the straight punch — or any punch for that matter. The leading straight punch is delivered from your ready stance without any added motions like drawing your hand back to your hip or shoulder, pulling back your shoulder, etc. Practice your lead punch from the ready stance and finish again in the ready stance (not back on the hip!). Later on, you should be able to strike from wherever the hand happens to be at the moment. Remember, punching in this manner will give you added

speed (no wasted motions) and deception (no give-away movements preceding the punch). [Use Zen illustration: Eat, but he is thinking; punch, but he is scared or rushing. Thus, a punch is not a punch.]

Most guarding is done with the rear hand — thus, the term "guarding hand." When striking with the lead hand, do not make the common mistake of the traditional, classical way by putting your rear hand on your hip. The rear hand is there to supplement your lead to make the attack a defensive offense. For example, when striking a body blow with the lead hand, the guarding hand (the rear hand) should be held high to offset any countering by your opponent to your upper body. In short, when one hand is out, the other should be either immobilizing one of the opponent's arms or withdrawing (not all the way to the hip!) for protection against countering and to secure a strategic position for a follow-up.

Relaxation is essential for faster and more powerful punching. Let your lead punch shoot out loosely and easily; do not tighten up or clench your fist until the moment of impact. All punches should end with a snap *several inches behind the target*. Thus, you punch *through* the opponent instead of *at* him.

All punches should end with a snap *several inches behind the target;* **punch** *through* **the opponent instead of** *at* **him.**

After shooting out the lead hand, do not drop it when withdrawing to the ready stance. Though you might see this being done by a good man because he is potentially fast and good at timing and distance, you should cultivate the habit of returning along the same path and keeping that hand high for any possible counters.

When striking with the lead hand, it is advisable to constantly vary the position of your head for added protection against the opponent's counter. During the first few inches of advancing, the head remains in line; after that, the head should adapt. Also, to minimize counters from the opponent, you should at times feint before leading. However, do not overdo the feinting or the headwork. *Remember* **simplicity;** *just enough is enough.*

Sometimes it pays to use double leads because they are unexpected and the second punch tends to disturb the opponent's rhythm and thus, paves the way for a follow-up.

When advancing to attack, the lead foot should not land before the fist makes contact or the body weight will end up on the floor instead of behind the punch. Remember to take up power from the ground by pushing off with the rear foot.

Your lead hand should be like greased lightning and must never be held rigidly or motionless. Keep it slightly moving (without exaggeration) in a threatening manner, as

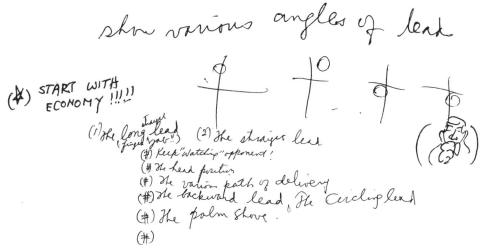

it not only keeps your opponent on edge, but also can be delivered faster from motion than from immobility. Like a cobra, your stroke should be felt before it is seen. This is particularly true of the leading finger jab.

THE ELUSIVE LEAD

In delivering the lead, the position of the head should be constantly varied, sometimes up, sometimes down, and sometimes "neither up nor down." Sometimes, the rear hand

Like a cobra, your stroke should be felt before it is seen.

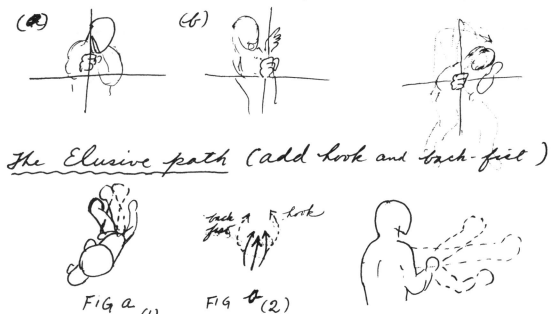

can be placed in front of face while leading. (This might entail a loss of reach and rapidity.) Keep your opponent guessing — variety — variety!

武道釋義

Straight hitting (and straight kicking) is the foundation of scientific fighting skill.

NOTE:

The Sudden Change of Level

Use the first two inches to lead, then a sudden change—head feint.

Use as defense for:

1. swings (hands feet)
2. hooks (hands feet)
3. reverse heels
4. spin kicks and blows.

Use to set-up for grappling and tackling.

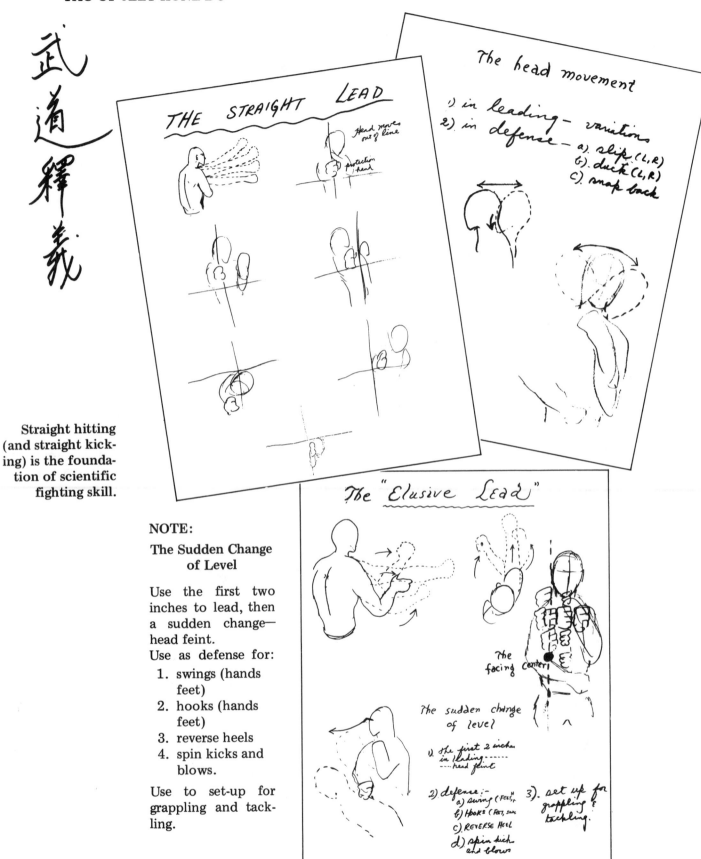

Necessary qualities of a straight lead:
1. Perfect balance of body.
2. Accuracy of aim.
3. Precise timing and coordination.
4. Maximum power of punch.

The straight lead is the blow that, whether used in attack or defense, leaves its exponent in hitting range for a shorter period than any other.

Most experts make it their principle blow.

Some fighters are continually making the alternating movements of engaging, then making an absence of touch (lowering or drifting the hand). This habit can be used to advantage. As the adversary is leaving the blade and moving across to the opposite line, the opportunity of making a straight thrust is present.

Straight hitting is based on an understanding of body structure and the value of leverage.

For an opponent who lacks decision, one who extends to lead but brings his hand back to the on-guard position, the straight thrust can follow advantageously.

The above defensive errors, in conjunction with a step forward by the opponent, render the straight thrust all the more possible.

Straight hitting (and straight kicking) is the foundation of scientific fighting skill. It developed late in history and, therefore, is the product of careful thought. Requiring speed and intelligence to use, it travels less distance than round arm blows (or hook and spin kicks) and will reach the mark first. Straight blows (and kicks) are more accurate than hooks and swings and allow full use of the arm (and leg) reach.

Straight hitting is based on an understanding of body structure and the value of leverage. It is an attempt to use body weight in every blow, hitting with the body and using the arms as merely the vehicles of force. Arm action alone is insufficient to give real power to blows. Real power, quick, accurate, can be obtained only by shifting the weight in such a manner that the hip and shoulder precede the arm to the center line of the body.

There are only two methods which obtain a complete shift of weight (compare this with kicking):

1. A pivot or quick turn of the waist, allowing the hip and shoulder to precede the arm.

2. A full body pivot, shifting the weight from one leg to the other.

———————————————

The waist pivot is faster and easier to learn and is used as a basis for teaching the art of hitting.

———————————————

Hitting does not mean *pushing*. True hitting may be likened to the snap of a whip — all the energy is slowly concentrated and then suddenly released with a tremendous outpouring of power. Pushing is exactly the opposite, with the concentrated force at the start of the blow and a subsequent loss of power as the arm leaves the body. In real hitting, the feet are always directly under the body. In pushing, the body is often off-balance as the force of the blow does not come from a *pivot* of the body but only from a push off the rear foot.

———————————————

Power in hitting comes from a quick twist of the waist, not a swinging, swaying movement.

Power in hitting comes from a *quick twist* of the waist, not a swinging, swaying movement, but a *pivot* over the straight lead leg. As long as this straight line is maintained, as long as the hips are relaxed and free to swing, as long as the shoulders are not tensed and are turned through to the center line of the body before the arms are extended, power will result and hitting will be an art.

———————————————

Once the *straight line* of the lead side of the body is broken, power is lost because the straight lead side of the body is the anchor, the pivot point, the hinge from which power and force is generated to its greatest height. So great is the power that may be attained in this manner that a real artist can deliver a knockout blow without taking a single step forward or displaying any apparent effort.

———————————————

Pay particular attention to the development of *relaxed tension*. If you tighten up, you lose the flexibility and timing which are so important to successful punches. Keep relaxed at all times and remember that timing is your chief aid in making a blow effective.

———————————————

Punches are not supposed to be thrown with a wind-up motion. They are made with a well-directed forearm and loose shoulder muscles. Only when the punch begins to land should the fist be clenched. The momentum helps carry the arm back to the proper position.

The top of your shoulder is at the *level* of the point you are striking. Sometimes it is all right to stand on the balls of your feet when landing a head shot on a tall person to make your shoulder come to the level of his jaw. When hitting to the pit of the stomach, both knees give way until the shoulder is at the level of the pit of the stomach.

Remember to *take up power from the ground* through your legs, waist and back. Sway all your muscles into your punches (at the same time do your best to cut down motions) and make them drive through. Push off from the ground.

When using a body pivot, turn on the balls of *both feet* while punching. The fist comes *straight* from the center with the full power of one or the other leg behind it. Sometimes a quick *three or four-inch* jump will do the trick.

According to your position and the time you have to put the right lead punch in, you may occasionally take a *short* step to the left, just a few inches, with your left foot (watch out for kicks). This will put even more weight into the punch, especially at fairly long range.

Take up power from the ground through your legs, waist and back.

Timing is best when the opponent rushes in.

Remember, when advancing the foot *must not land first* or the body weight will rest upon the floor instead of being behind the punch — heel slightly raised and pointing outward.

Always have the legs slightly bent so that the strong thigh muscles come into play (like a spring), especially before coming in.

Your step should be long enough to make your reach good and you should drive your punch slightly through your target. *Use your whole reach!*

To ensure success, the straight hit and the lunge (step) must be one coordinated move.

Your head should sway slightly to the right as it moves forward with your step.

Endeavor never to flinch or close your eyes, but watch your opponent intently all the time. Keep your chin firmly set and nicely tucked away.

Remember the "covered line" (outside or in) and the supplementary guard, always there corresponding to the uncovered line.

Always keep the rear hand guard up! Be ready to follow with the rear hand.

Follow-Through

First of all, there are different types of force applications and one should use all of them.

There are different types of force applications and one should use all of them.

Follow-through generally refers to continuation of a high rate of movement, or even an acceleration from the instant of contact, until the ceasing of contact. The punch should increase in speed throughout its run and when it lands, still have enough momentum and power to drive *clear through* the object. Do not aim merely to strike *at* your man; aim to drive *through* him — but do not have a "lean on" effect!

Make up your *mind* that you'll hit as hard as you possibly can with every ounce of your bodily strength, with every fiber of your mental determination, and also that you'll keep on hitting harder and harder as you progress through the object.

In boxing, for example, the athlete is taught to "strike through" the opponent — to maintain or increase the rate of movement during the contact so that the "explosive push" carries through farther and changes the opponent's position more sharply.

Wrist snaps at the last instant in striking acts are last moment accelerations that literally *go into* the object (i.e.: compressed tennis ball). Instead of a relaxing follow-through, the fighter must bring his hands back as fast as he thrusts them out. Reversing the waist movement aids in last minute acceleration as well as return.

Lead to Body

A lead to the body is an effective blow used to bother the opponent and bring down his guard (as the preceding feint of a high lead).

While not ordinarily a hard blow, it can cause distress if driven to the solar plexus. It is important that the body follow the arm. In other words, a blow to the body is more effective and safer if the executioner sinks to the level of the target.

Drop the body forward from the waist to a position at right angles to the legs. Keep the forward leg only slightly bent but the rear leg more completely flexed. As the body drops, drive the lead arm into forceful extension toward the opponent's solar plexus. *The blow is slightly upward, never downward.* The rear hand is carried high in front of the body, ready for the opponent's leading hook. Hold the head down so that only the top is visible and will be protected by the extended punching arm. The head should be held tight against the extended arm.

To hit with a straight right lead to the body, feint with the left hand toward the head by extending the left hand quickly with a slight forward movement. Step well in with the left foot (keeping it still in the rear), and at the same time lean over to the left side. You will be practically clear of all danger. The right that follows can become a punishing hit and one difficult to deal with. Furthermore, you are in a position to bring up the left to the head with great force.

The whole secret of the actual force of a terrific punch is its timing, coordinated, of course, with the accuracy of its aim.

Training Aids

It is most important, after recovering to a boxing position from any set maneuver (executed on count or "as you will"), to shuffle about a few seconds on the balls of your feet for footwork drill and relaxation before repeating the set maneuver. This tactic deftly simulates actual fighting within the drill.

The whole secret of the actual force of a terrific punch is its timing, coordinated, of course, with the accuracy of its aim. Hang a small ball to practice aim.

Practice shooting the lead out in a quick succession of blows, withdrawing the striking arm just sufficient so as to enable full power to be put behind each blow.

Learn economical motion of delivery from a variety of angles, then lengthen the distance gradually.

One important point: In all **hand** *techniques, the hand moves first, preceding the foot. Keep this in mind —* **hand before foot** *— always.*

Defenses for a Straight Lead

The following are examples of defenses against a straight lead while in a right stance:

\# Have the left hand ready in anticipation of a lead. It is already opened, held a little higher than usual and weaves in controlled circles in front of your body. Immediately, the lead hand of your opponent flickers on its way to your face. Lean slightly to the left and strike firmly and quickly at his wrist or forearm with your left hand — no strength whatever is required to deflect the heaviest blow this way. Don't fail to take advantage of the opening. Put in a stiff lead to the face or body. Your opponent will be both off-guard and off-balance.

\# Sway to the left, stepping in with the right foot and deliver a severe body shot with your right hand. (This may be varied by a punch to the face.)

\# Sway to the right, stepping in with the right foot and deliver a heavy left-hand punch to the body (or head in a cross-counter).

\# Snap back, then forward with a return.

––––––––––––––––––––

The lead jab is a "feeler." It is the basis of all other blows, a loose, easy stinger.

One should always finish punching with his lead hand to enable him to return to the correct fighting position instantly.

––––––––––––––––––––

Vary the leads to the head and body.

––––––––––––––––––––

LEAD JAB

The lead jab is a "feeler." It is the basis of all other blows, a loose, easy stinger. It is a whip rather than a club. Ali's theory is to picture hitting a fly with a swatter.

––––––––––––––––––––

Its great advantage is that body balance is not disturbed and it is both an offensive and a defensive weapon. In offense, the lead jab serves to keep your opponent off-balance and paves the way for more severe punching. When used as a defensive blow, the jab often stops or effectively meets an attack. You can frequently slip in a sudden and disconcerting jab to the other fellow's face at the very moment he is *about to let go* a real punch at you. Used correctly, it is the sign of the scientific fighter, who uses strategy rather than force. It requires skill and finesse as well as speed and deception (broken rhythm). Keep in mind that there is nothing worse than a slow jab, except one which is telegraphed.

––––––––––––––––––––

It is important that, upon shooting your lead jab, you instantly return your fist to its on-guard position, ready to punch again or to protect yourself from a counterpunch.

The jab is snapped across, not pushed, and should be brought back high and kept high to offset a rear-hand counter. The arms merely relax and sink back to the body rather than being pulled back. This is as important as knowing how to deliver.

At the time of landing the jab, the chin is tucked down and the shoulder is curved around the chin as a protective covering.

In all hitting, including the lead jab, all force is outward from the body. The movement of the lead jab should be a continuous winding motion from the shoulder.

It is often advisable to shoot more than one jab. The second jab has an excellent chance of landing (providing the first one was delivered with utmost economy) and it also serves to cover up the missed first jab. Of course, you should shoot as many more as you wish.

Continue to practice the jab until it is a light, easy, natural movement. Carry the shoulder and arm relaxed and ready at all times. It requires long, diligent practice to make the movement *automatic* and to obtain speed and power *without apparent effort*. Accuracy should be the main objective and the straighter you jab, the better.

In all hitting, including the lead jab, all force is outward from the body.

If you cannot get at the opponent's head or body, aim at his bicep.

The jab may also be effectively used with the fist closed to *stiff-arm* the opponent away from you in defense.

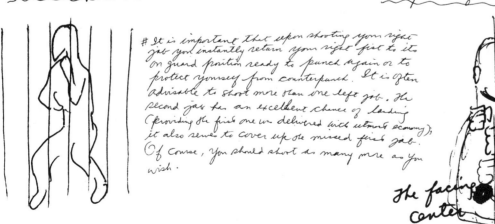

The economy base

The paths of leading

It is important that upon shooting your right jab you instantly return your right fist to its on guard position ready to punch again or to protect yourself from counterpunch. It is often advisable to shoot more than one left jab. The second jab has an excellent chance of landing (providing the first one was delivered with utmost economy); it also serves to cover up the missed first jab. Of course, you should shoot as many more as you wish.

The facing center

Keep him on the defensive and increase the pace ever so steadily. Give him no rest.

LEADING FINGER JAB

Like a fencer's sword that is always in line, the leading finger jab is a constant threat to your opponent. Basically, it is Western sword fencing without a sword and the primary target is your opponent's eyes.

The leading finger jab is the longest of all hand weapons as well as the fastest because of the little force needed. You do not need power to jab at an opponent's eyes. Rather, the ability to seize an opportunity with accuracy and speed is the main thing in the efficient use of the finger jab. Thus, as in all hand techniques, the finger jab should begin from your ready position without any added motions. It starts from your ready position and back again, like greased lightning. Like a cobra, your finger jab should be felt and not seen.

You should be able to snap, not push, the finger jab out singly or in combination. Unless you are naturally fast, your opponent will many times be able to avoid one finger jab but you will usually catch him by instantly following the first with a second. The leading finger jab is one of the most efficient weapons, especially in self-defense, and should be cultivated to the highest form of proficiency.

Due to the fact that you use *shocking flickering force* rather than punching force, the leading finger jab also (with the point of view on jabbing) is like swatting a fly. Accuracy is what counts. Choose your target *during movement* and *let go* to recover with ready reinforcements.

Training Aids

Practice and sharpen your finger jab *when you are fresh* or you will begin to substitute gross motions for fine ones and generalized efforts for specific economical ones. Leave endurance exercises until *after* skill training.

1. "A" and "B" face each other in a ready position.

2. "A" advances with a low shin kick. This is mainly used as a feint to disturb the opponent's composure and lengthen his reaction time. It also serves to obstruct any possible kick during the advance.

3. As soon as the distance is bridged and slightly before "A's" lead foot is down alongside "B's" foot, A whips out his finger jab straight as an arrow to "B's" now opened guard.

Reread the descriptions on the straight lead.

The finger jab is Western sword fencing without a sword and the primary target is your opponent's eyes.

STRAIGHT REAR THRUST TO BODY

The straight rear thrust to the body is a power blow and used either as a counter or after a preliminary feint with the leading hand. As in the leading jab to the body, the body follows the blow (keep a good defensive position — watch out for a hammer blow counter), although added force can be obtained by a body pivot to a position over the lead foot. (Examine the difference between the two.) It is effective in pulling down an opponent's guard and can be used with great success against the tall fighter.

———————————————————

This blow should be used more frequently. When properly timed and correctly delivered, it is a most punishing blow and a comparatively safe one, since you crouch as you drive the punch home, thus avoiding full-arm counters. Opportunities for the use of this blow are rather frequent, since it is one of the best counters to the opponent's opposite lead, which exposes one side of his body.

———————————————————

The front hand is up and open, elbow down, guarding against the opponent's rear hand. The head is down along the punching arm and, thus, well-protected.

> When properly timed and correctly delivered, the straight rear thrust to the body is a most punishing blow and a comparatively safe one.

———————————————————

This blow should be frequently employed against an adversary who protects his *face* with the rear hand when "leading" to the head.

———————————————————

You have a foot of body to shoot at for each inch of chin. Also, the body is less mobile.

———————————————————

Delivering a straight rear thrust to the body: Feint with your lead hand at the head and "draw" your opponent's lead as a counter to your feint, or else, wait for him to lead.

———————————————————

Stopping a straight rear thrust to the body: Merely press your front arm across your body. At the same time, raise your lead shoulder for fear the body blow turns into a double hit — "loop hit."

———————————————————

REAR CROSS

In your on-guard position, your rear fist is cocked somewhere under your chin, an inch or two out from your chest. When you hit with your lead, the twist at your waist shifts your rear fist from its regular on-guard position, back four or five inches to a point from which you can, without telegraphing or drawing back, hit one of the hardest blows in boxing, the rear cross.

The rear cross is delivered in much the same manner as the lead jab in that it travels in a perfectly straight line. The rear cross, however, is the heavy artillery and the twist at your waist will be much greater.

―――――――――――――――――――

In any power blow, the bone structure must be aligned so as to form one straight body side or line which enables it to support the weight of the body, thus freeing the muscles to propel the other side of the body forward and create terrific force. *One side of the body must always form a straight line.*

―――――――――――――――――――

It is important to make sure your rear heel and rear shoulder turn in one piece. This is accomplished by merely shifting the body weight over a straight lead leg, hinging the lead side of the body and freeing the opposite side for a forceful turn or explosive pivot. It is the same idea as in slamming a door.

―――――――――――――――――――

Your weight should begin on the ball of your rear foot. As your rear fist travels, it twists and your rear shoulder moves into the blow. You twist at the waist and the weight of your body is shifted forward into the punch and to your lead foot *before connecting.* Your rear foot follows by dragging forward a few inches in the direction of the punch and your lead fist shifts back as your body twists.

The rear cross is the heavy artillery.

―――――――――――――――――――

Remember, the secret of power in the straight rear cross (or thrust) is using the lead side of the body as a hinge and allowing the rear side of the body to swing free.

―――――――――――――――――――

Let the blow slip out loose and easy, don't grip, don't tighten up the arm at the beginning of the punch — let the contraction of the muscles come just as the blow lands, with a last closing and tightening on the fist, a final burst of nervous energy to drive *through* the opponent. Its force depends on speed (and more speed) and *timing* with the opponent's movements. Do not forget the *drive* from the rear leg.

―――――――――――――――――――

Keep your hands well up at all times; especially don't drop the rear hand while punching with the lead. Blows should start where the hands are. The start is normally made from the on-guard position with no preliminary movement, no lifting or drawing back. The shoulder curves over the chin for protection and the chin is down. The rear hand must be shot from its "resting place" on the chest or body; it generally starts from near the rear shoulder.

―――――――――――――――――――

As the rear arm is extended, the lead arm is held close to the side in the position of guard. This is done not only for an expected counter, but also so the boxer will be in position to throw the second follow-up punch. *Remember,* one hand out, one hand back. This movement must be practiced until it can be easily, quickly and correctly performed. The arm should drive out with such snapping force as would seem to pull it clear of the socket. Again, the blow must be driven *through*, not just at, an object. The arm then relaxes back to the on-guard position.

When using the rear cross, you must not hesitate. If you think you have the opening, you should let it fly and not be half-hearted about it.

Because the rear cross is a long-range blow, to be effective it must be delivered straight as an arrow, fast as a shot and completely without warning. The most important part of the rear cross is to cultivate a delivery speed so, when you strike, the damage is done before your opponent realizes it. You must also be *accurate* with the straight rear cross — far more accurate than your lead — and the straighter you keep the cross, the more accurate and the more *explosive* it will be.

Unless you have *correct balance*, you will not be in a position to deliver a lead shot after your rear cross. This is most important, because if your opponent ducks to avoid the rear cross, your *quickest method of recovery* is to throw a lead and you must be in a correct position to do so. If you are trying to correct faulty footwork in those split seconds, you may well find yourself flat on your back.

> If you think you have the opening, you should let fly and not be half-hearted about it.

The rear cross is difficult to use because the rear hand has farther to travel and use of the rear hand will present an opening for your opponent if you miss. Practice minimizing the above two points and, thus, perfect the rear cross — non-telegraphic starting, quick recovery.

In a Right Stance

Usually, you will hit with your left fist after first having shot a right (one-two).

Keep the right hand *moving;* don't hold it motionless. Let it flicker in and out like the tongue of a snake ready to strike. Above all, always threaten and worry your adversary.

Throw the right out, stepping out with the right foot simultaneously. Before it reaches its mark (blocking the sight of the opponent), drive your left fist straight out (without pulling it back even a fraction) and twist your body to the right, pivoting on the sole of your left foot. As you pivot, get plenty of push and snap from the left side of your

body, up from the foot, through the legs and hips, and make sure it is capped off by plenty of snap from your left shoulder. This power is accentuated by the *coordination* of the whole body in the follow-through. Keep balanced at all times.

It should be noted that the left (or rear) thrust is often a counterblow. Sometimes it is better to *feint the opponent into leading* to shoot the left as a counter. Here the blow is delivered perfectly straight during the opponent's lead at your face. You step inside a right lead, allowing it to slip over your left shoulder, and shoot the left, meanwhile keeping an eye on his left or putting a stop to it with your right. Your head must be ducked forward and to the right, to avoid the opponent's right lead (keep your eyes on him!), but the duck must be very slight, just sufficient to avoid being hit. The left hand, back uppermost, should just skim the opponent's elbow before his lead is straightened and the swing of the body on the hips, from left to right, should be assisted by jerking back the right elbow and shoulder.

Power is accentuated by the *coordination* of the whole body in the follow-through.

It generally meets your man coming in and lands on the angle of the jaw. Do not always hit at the head, however. Aim toward the center line to drive *through* the opponent.

Try a left to the stomach, then left cross.
Try two right leads to time your left straight.

Sometimes, move over a little further to the right and shoot the straight left *inside* his arm in a *slight upward direction*.

When returning, keep your lead shoulder raised for a right stancer's left cross or a left stancer's lead hook.

In-fighting — Short Man Versus Tall Man

Keep your hands up, elbows close to your body. Bob and weave, moving from side to side. Gauge your opponent's leads — make him miss and *get inside* his punches by ducking, slipping, feinting or "sticking" with controlling hands. A short, straight left, rather than a hard, telegraphed one will do the trick. The opportunity is usually there but only for an instant — hence, the short, fast left, rather than the looping, hard left.

Capitalize on a hooker who either drops the hook upon delivery or throws it in too wide

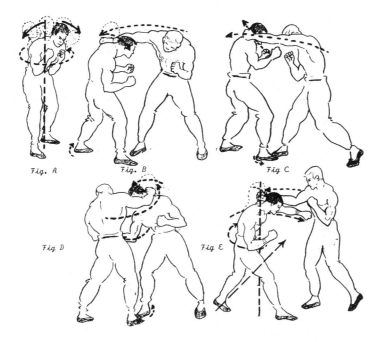

an arc. You should shoot over a hard straight left as soon as his right shoulder is lowered or the wide arc begins.

The overhand left is used by small fellows against taller men. It travels in a circular

Capitalize on a hooker who either drops the hook upon delivery or throws it in too wide an arc.

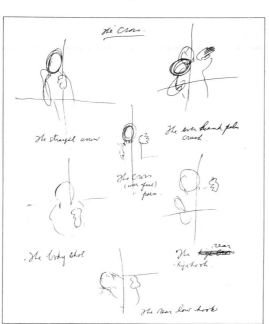

"over" motion into the vicinity of the opposition's head. The movement must come from the shoulder. Vary it with an inward palm stroke.

Always try to nail a medium-range target (body or head) with stepping straight punches. However, if your opponent is blocking, evading or countering those straight blows, you can resort to medium-range hooking attempts.

THE HOOK

The hook is more effective as a counterblow. It is never a wide, looping blow, but is more like a loose, easy, snappy punch. Remember, the pivot is the key; footwork makes the punch.

Avoid telegraphing! Start and end in the ready position. It must begin from the on-guard position for proper deception. The hand is never pulled back or lowered. Always jab or feint first to get your distance and leverage.

When using a lead hook, always keep your rear hand high as a shield for your face. Your rear elbow protects your ribs on that side.

The hook is mastered chiefly on the small punching bag. Try to explode sharply without twisting the body out of shape and be ready to follow-up with more punches.

LEAD HOOK

The more versatile the fighter — the more alert mentally and the more agile physically — the more apt he is to shove the most unorthodox blows from the most impossible angles.

The lead hook should be used *judiciously*. It is most effective when going in or coming out and is useful against an over-reaching straight or against swings.

With the opponent in the same stance, the lead hook is often delivered when he has lowered his rear hand guard or after he has executed a lead jab.

Against a clever defensive fighter, the lead hook is sometimes the only way you can penetrate his defense or force him to vary it so that you can find openings for other types of punches.

The lead hook can be used *as a lead* when, for some reason, your opponent has lost his ability to move out of the way. It is more effective as a counterblow or as a follow-up, however, because it is basically a short-range weapon — when the opponent is coming to you. Try a straight lead or some other preparation first. A good way to use the lead hook powerfully is to fake a rear cross. Always vary your punches: high/low or low/high, singly or in combination. Jabbing and feinting (with advance) is a good means of getting your distance.

The lead hook is also a good punch while in-fighting — it comes from the side, outside the range of vision, as it were, and will go *around* the guard. This is valuable when close in, especially after the opponent is shaken up by a straight blow.

The body is the easier target for the simple reason it covers a far larger surface than the jaw and is less mobile. The groin might be a better target, too, and is definitely harder to block than the jaw.

A hook to the body is more effective close in. Feint to his head, then, in a flash, step forward with the lead foot and sink your lead hook into his stomach, ribs, groin or whichever target is closer. At the same time, duck to the *opposite* side from which your hook is being thrown. In doing this, you must bend your lead knee, bringing your shoulder as near as possible, level with the striking point. To preserve balance, turn the *toe* of the rear foot well out. *Keep your rear guard up.*

The body is the easier target for the simple reason it covers a far larger surface than the jaw and is less mobile.

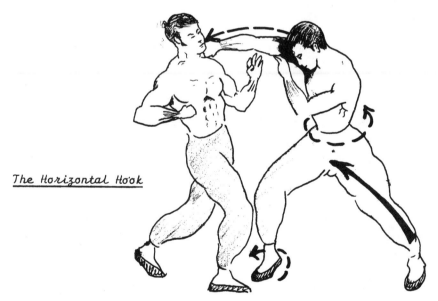

The Horizontal Hook

The hook is a good punch to combine with a sidestep, for you are moving sideways and it is the natural way to swing at that moment. Similarly, you may land effectively on your opponent with a hook at the instant he is trying to sidestep. Remember, if you catch your man *coming in*, the blow will be twice as hard. Remember, also, to *keep your rear hand up while striking!*

According to Mills, there are at least two ways to deliver a lead hook.

The long lead hook: Stab your opponent's face with a straight lead and quickly follow with the hook. (Study the weight shift in attacking and countering — reaching forward and shifting to the back leg.)

The short lead hook: This is delivered from the on-guard position with the elbow closer to your side. (As you counter, shift your weight from the lead to the rear.)

Like all punches, the lead hook must begin from the on-guard position for added deception.

Always jab or feint first to get distance. For example, feint a cross to prepare leverage but don't throw it too far. Most boxers pull their hand back too far before throwing the hook. Try not to pull or lower the hand. Enough power can be put into the punch *without* pulling the arm far back. Much of the "kick" behind the lead hook is accomplished by the footwork.

Remember that punches are not supposed to be thrown with a wind-up motion.

The lead heel must be raised outward so that the body can pivot, and the waist and shoulders reverse when the blow lands.

You should keep the lead shoulder high for full leverage when you hook to the side of the chin.

Remember that punches are not supposed to be thrown with a wind-up motion. They are made with a well-directed forearm and loose shoulder muscles. The momentum helps carry the arm back to the proper position.

Frequently, a boxer tries to put too much body behind the punch, thereby making it a push punch. The hook is a loose, arm-propelled punch. The "kick" comes from the looseness of the delivery and the proper pivoting of the feet and body. The weight of the body is shifted with the hook to the side opposite the side you hook from. If you lead a hook, you must step in with the punch to make your reach good. Use a loose, easy, snappy punch; never a wide and looping blow.

In loose hooking, the whip of the arm is caused by turning the body away from the arm until the range of movement in the shoulder joint is completely used. Then, the arm must turn with the body. Executed quickly, this causes the arm to whip forward as if released from a bow. Make the blow *snappy*; always think of speed and *more speed*. Aim to drive *through* the opponent.

Your lead heel is raised outward, *swiveling* on the ball of your lead foot so that your blow will have a better reach and will go *through* better and faster. Drop a little to the opposite side to get more weight *and to safeguard yourself.*

Above all, *minimize* all motion so that you will be moving just enough to have the maximum effect without hooking wildly.

The more you "open" an outside hook, the more it degenerates into a swing. You must keep it tight. Also, when you open a hook, you open your own defense.

The great difficulty is in learning to swing sharply without twisting the body out of shape.

Above all, minimize all motion so that you will be moving just enough to have the maximum effect.

The more sharply the elbow is bent, the tighter and more explosive the hook. Experiment with the arm slightly rigid prior to landing.

There are no wrists in boxing. (Experiment with that statement.) The forearm and the fist should be used as one solid piece, like a club with a knot on the end of it. The fist should be kept on a straight line with the forearm and there should be no bending of the wrist in any direction. Be careful not to hit with your thumb.

At the finish of the punch, the thumb is up. There is no twist of the fist — for proper protection of the hand. The forearm is rigid from the elbow to the knuckles and does not bend at the wrist. Remember always that your knuckles are pointing in the exact direction of your whirling weight.

Always keep the rear hand high as a shield for the other side of your face. The rear elbow protects the ribs. Make both points a habit!

Be ready to follow-up with another solid punch *with either hand.*

When blocking a hook, the tendency is to pull away or out from the blow. This is absolutely the wrong thing to do. *Move in, not out,* so that the hook ends harmlessly around your neck.

The hook is mastered chiefly on the small speed bag; try to explode sharply without twisting your body out of shape. Be sure your fists feel comfortable.

REAR HOOK

The rear hook is valuable for in-fighting, especially when coming away on the break or when the opponent is backing away. Sometimes, you can take your opponent's attention off the lead hook by showing him your rear punch.

Study a left rear hook to the kidney of a crouching opposition, an opponent who turns constantly in a right stance to the left, leaving his right kidney an open target. The fist is looped in a half-circle into the kidney.

The hook is mastered chiefly on the small speed bag.

SHOVEL HOOK

Shovel hooks are thrown "inside" with the elbows *in,* pressing tightly against the hips for body blows and pressing tightly against the lower ribs for head blows. They are thrown from your on-guard position and they are short-range dandies. Make certain you have no tension in the elbow, shoulder or legs until the whirl is started. Your hip comes up in a vigorous shoveling hunch and your hand is at a 45-degree angle. The punch is angled to shoot inside an opponent's defense.

Execution (right stance): Pull your right elbow *in* and press it firmly against the *front* edge of your hip bone. Turn your half-opened right hand up slightly so that your palm is partially facing the ceiling. Your palm should slant at an angle of about 45 degrees with the floor and ceiling. Meanwhile, keep your left guard in normal position. Now, without moving your feet, suddenly whirl your body to your left in such fashion that your right hip comes up with a circling, shoveling hunch that sends your exploding right fist solidly into the target about solar plexus high. The slanting angle of your right hand permits you to land solidly with your striking knuckles. Make certain you have no tension in your elbow, shoulder or legs until the whirl is started from your normal position. More important, make certain that your hand is at the 45-degree angle and your hip comes up in a vigorous shoveling hunch.

The *fist angle* and the *hip hunch* are important features of all shovel hooks, whether to the body or head. The leg spring used in the hip hunch speeds up your body whirl and, at the same time, deflects the direction of the whirl slightly upward in a surge. Meanwhile, the combination of the angled fist and the bent elbow points your striking knuckles in the same direction as that of the whirling surge. You have a *pure* punch. Your fist lands with a solid smash that packs plenty of follow-through. And your pure punch is *angled* to shoot *inside* an opponent's defenses.

Shovels to the head are delivered from the on-guard position. (Better practice it on the speed bag.) Fold your right arm in toward your body, keeping your forearm straight up until your thumb knuckle is only a slight distance from your right shoulder. Be sure that your right elbow is well *in* and that it is pressing against your lower right ribs. Now, without moving your feet, suddenly give your body the combination shoulder whirl and hip hunch and let your angled right fist explode the punch against your chin-high target. Make certain each time that your elbow is pressing against your lower ribs at the start of the whirl and that your fist, when it lands, is only a short distance from your right shoulder.

Shovel hooks are full-fledged inside lead hooks, one of the *shortest*, yet one of the most explosive blows. Once you have mastered it, your hands will flash instinctively to their shovel post as your body starts its hunching whirl. *Your body will pick them up.*

> Your pure punch is *angled* to shoot *inside* an opponent's defenses.

You can make the range with any number of attack combinations in which the shovels are used for follow shots. The simplest combinations would be a long right jolt to the head (from a right stance), which failed to knock your opponent backward, followed immediately by a *left* shovel to the head or body. Or, you could follow a similar straight right to the head with a right shovel to the head or body. Likewise, a long straight *left* to the head, which failed to accomplish its explosive object, would put you in position for right shovels to either target. Also, if a fast opponent steps into you, his speed may be such that you can't catch him with a stepping counterpunch, but that very speed may make him a perfect "clay pigeon" for your short-range artillery. In addition, you'll be in short range for *counter-shovels* many times when you ward off attacks by means of blocks, parries, slips and the like.

The shovel ranks next to your long, straight punches (according to Dempsey). They enable you to knock out or at least soften up an opponent who is trying to clinch with you. (Don't forget to use elbows, stomps, knees.) They help you to keep *inside* the attack of bobbing weavers, most of whom hook from the *outside*, and help you straighten them up. Since the shovels are all short, tight blows, you are less likely to get hit while using them than while throwing the more open *outside* hook.

CORKSCREW HOOK

Strictly speaking, a corkscrew hook is delivered almost like a straight punch with the difference that, just before contact, the wrist is turned sharply. It is a curved, tearing, knuckle jab for medium range.

———————————

The essence of any hook is that the striker raises his elbow at the last possible moment when swinging. This will bring his knuckles around so they will make contact when his punch lands.

———————————

Execution (right stance): From your on-guard position, start your shoulder whirl as if you were going to shoot a medium-range right jab — no preparatory movement. Instead of jabbing, however, snap your right forearm and fist down, and your right elbow up. Your right fist snaps down with a screwing motion that causes your striking knuckles to land properly on the target. When your fist explodes against the target, your forearm is almost parallel to the floor.

———————————

The essence of any hook is that the striker raises his elbow at the last possible moment when swinging.

When you step in with the right corkscrew, you move in with a "pivot step" — stepping forward and slightly to your own right, pointing the toe sharply in. Your body pivots on the ball of your right foot as your right arm and fist snap down to the target. At the instant of the fist's landing, your rear left foot generally is in the air, but it settles immediately behind you.

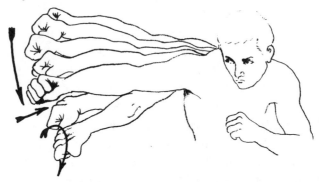

If you have a potent right corkscrew that *flashes in without warning*, your opponent will be very cautious about menacing you with his rear left fist. You can use the corkscrew hook to beat an adversary's rear cross. Moreover, if he permits his guarding left hand to creep too far forward as he blocks or parries your leading right jab, your corkscrew hook can snap down *behind* that guarding left and nail his jaw.

———————————

The right corkscrew is often delivered while you are circling to your opponent's left.

———————————

Practice on the light speed bag to obtain proper form and zip.

PALM HOOK

The palm hook is simply a fast, open hand hook that hits with the palm of the hand.

In the normal punching position, the right outside palm hook is very useful as a lead that shoots in *behind* the opponent's guarding rear hand. And, it is useful as a counter that, with guarding or slipping, beats a straight lead to the punch.

UPPERCUT

Lead and rear hand uppercuts are used freely in close-quarter work. There are many opportunities for the punch once you get the inside position.

Uppercuts can be used for head down charges and wild swinging blows. This presupposes that you do not go in with your head down or body bent forward until you have thoroughly sized up your opponent's style or you will run into an uppercut.

The uppercut becomes almost useless against a fast boxer who stands upright all the time and simply jabs a long lead in your face.

The short uppercut is an effective one. Keep your legs bent before striking; straighten them suddenly as you send the punch in. Get up on your toes and lean back a little as the blow lands, dropping more weight on the left leg when using the right and more on the right leg when using the left.

Against a right stancer, when uppercutting with the lead right hand, lay your left hand for a moment on your opponent's right shoulder to make sure you don't run into a heavy return.

Rear hand uppercut (right stance): Draw a right lead, then step in with a quick head twist to the right. As he's still leaning forward in his lead, deliver a short, sharp, left uppercut to his chin, raising and obstructing his right with your punching arm.

The left rear uppercut is delivered by lowering the left *on the way across* and "scooping" up and to the jaw or groin. The lead hand is drawn back for protection as well as strategic offensive position.

The uppercut becomes almost useless against a fast boxer who stands upright all the time and simply jabs a long lead in your face. You must then plan to get to close-

quarters and apply this punch to his groin, etc. By these methods, you may then tire him so much that he will drop his head.

———————————————

The blow may be practiced upon a hanging bag of Indian corn.

———————————————

a) Upward hook: You screw the blow up and in so that you can send it to the chin of a man who covers his face by holding his arm across it. Use a violent turn of the hip. (Note descriptions of the *corkscrew hook.*)

b) Horizontal hook — Forward hook: Both go over or around the man's guard. It's almost a bent-arm jab. Drive through with the body. (Note descriptions of the *shovel hook.*)

Hit as straight as possible. *Don't telegraph any punch.*

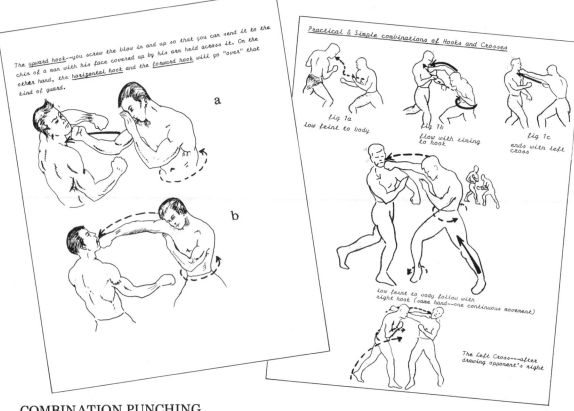

COMBINATION PUNCHING

A good Western boxer hits from every angle. *Each punch sets him in position to deliver another punch.* He is always on center, never off-balance. The more effective combinations a fighter has, the more different types of opponents he will be able to defeat.

———————————————

Some observations are applicable to all types of hitting. *Hit as straight as possible.* Step in when you punch and make your reach good. *Don't telegraph any punch.* If you have to set your fist in a certain way for a particular punch, do it in a manner that won't warn your opponent. *Fight from a center and always be in position and balanced to shoot any punch.* Don't overshoot your target. *After hitting, instantly get back on guard. End a series of punches with your lead hand.*

For long-range fighting, jab with your lead and cross with your rear. For short-range fighting use hooks, rear hand body blows and uppercuts.

Sway a little as you hit. A hard punch must be delivered from a solid base; light punches are delivered by a boxer on his toes.

Learn to hold your fire until you can hit your opponent. Back him to the ropes or corner him before you attack. Don't waste your energy missing. If he does the leading, avoid his punches and hit back with solid counterpunches before he can get away.

Learn to hold your fire until you can hit your opponent.

Keep loose and relaxed except when actually fighting. Develop speed, timing and judgment of distance by many hard workouts with all types of sparring partners. With this, practice your authority; hit confidently and hard.

GRAPPLING

Throwing

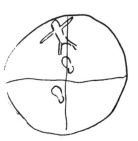

1. Hooking throw
2. Reverse hooking throw
3. Single leg tackle and trip
4. Double leg tackle
5. Right foot sweep — with or without arm drag to right or left stance
6. Left foot sweep — with or without arm drag to right or left stance
7. Kick back

Joint Locks

Joint locks may be done while standing or lying on the ground, as an immobilizing technique.

1. Outside armpit lock — to left or right stance
2. Wrist lock
3. Reverse wrist lock
4. Reverse twisting wrist lock — to double arm lock
5. Lying across arm bar
6. Standing single leg lock
7. Lying single leg lock
8. Single leg and spine lock
9. Double leg and spine lock
10. Foot twist toe hold

Chokes

1. Rear drop choke
2. Lean over drop choke
3. Side drop choke

Foul Tactics

1. Hair pulling while in-fighting . . . . for control
2. Foot stomp while in-fighting . . . . for maiming
3. Skin pinching, biting and ear pulling . . . . . for release or control
4. Groin grabbing . . . . for maiming or release

Gauge your opponent's leads — make him miss and *get inside* his punches by ducking, slipping, feinting or "sticking" with controlling hands.

Takedown Methods

1. Circle step single leg tackle
2. Drop step leg tackle
3. Draw step leg tackle

(1)  (2)  (3)

Do's

1. Always keep moving.
2. Be prepared for counters.
3. Develop cat-like movements.
4. Make the opponent wrestle your way.
5. Be aggressive; make your opponent think defense.

Don'ts

1. Don't cross your legs
2. Don't commit your arms too deeply.
3. Don't chase your opponent.
4. Don't rely on one takedown; be ready for other openings.
5. Don't let your opponent circle you.

DOUBLE LEG ATTACKS

LEG ATTACKS ;— a). The double leg attack
b). The single " "

a). The Double leg attack ;— a). The back heel (groin punch)
b). The follow through lift
(back stomp)

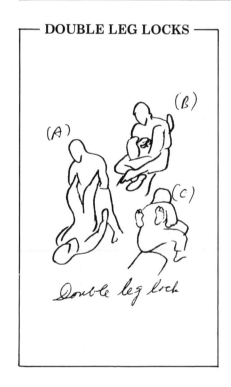

DOUBLE LEG LOCKS

(A) (B)
(C)

Double leg lock

SINGLE LEG ATTACKS

b) Single leg attack

1) The back trip to groin strike

2) The forward trip to side strangulation

3) The smash and groin strike

④ snap (捕!) and heel to leg lock

to groin strike

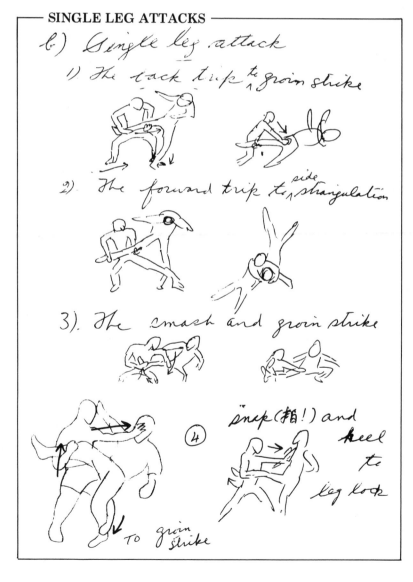

The elements
of attack are
all used to carry
the attack through
strategy, requiring
speed, deception,
timing and
judgment.

SINGLE LEG LOCKS

single leg lock
(A)

free leg to spread leg
knee or kick to groin

(B)

(C)

TO TOE HOLD

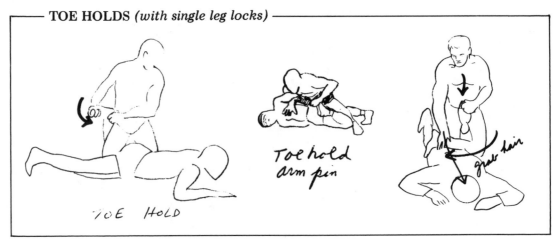

TOE HOLDS *(with single leg locks)*

TOE HOLD

Toe hold
arm pin

grab hair

SINGLE LEG TAKEDOWN and LOCK

ankle pick up
with thrust to
groin + foot twist → leg lock.

ELBOW THROW-BYS

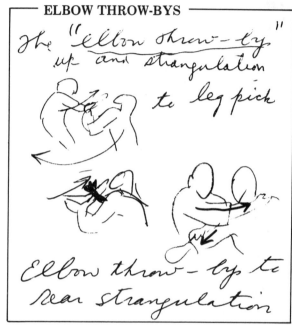

The "Elbow throw-bys"
up and strangulation
to leg pick

Elbow throw-bys to
Rear strangulation

ARM BLAST

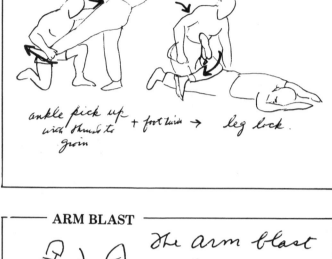

The arm blast
leg attach to
groin squeeze

ARM DRAG

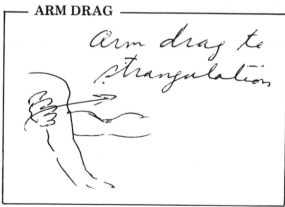

Arm drag to
strangulation

WRIST PASS

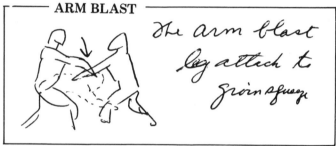

The wrist
post

TOUCH (JAB) and GO

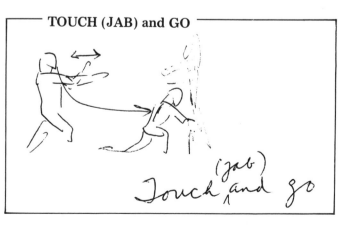

Touch (jab) and go

Feints are really decoys and if the opponent attempts to adjust his defense, the expert takes advantage of the openings created.

HEAD and NECK MANIPULATIONS

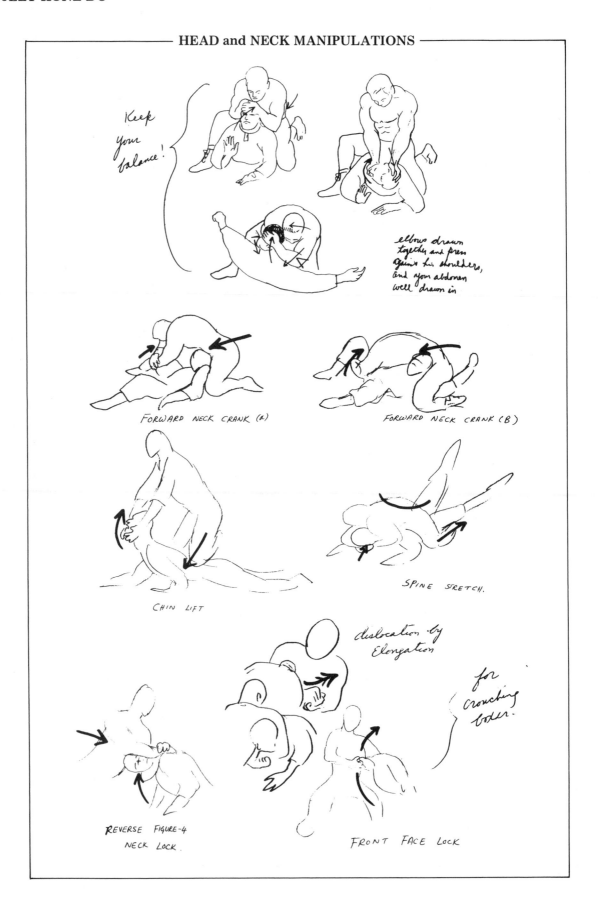

Keep your balance!

elbows drawn together and press against his shoulders, and your abdomen well drawn in

FORWARD NECK CRANK (A)

FORWARD NECK CRANK (B)

CHIN LIFT

SPINE STRETCH.

dislocation by Elongation

for crouching boxer.

REVERSE FIGURE-4 NECK LOCK.

FRONT FACE LOCK

HEAD and NECK MANIPULATIONS

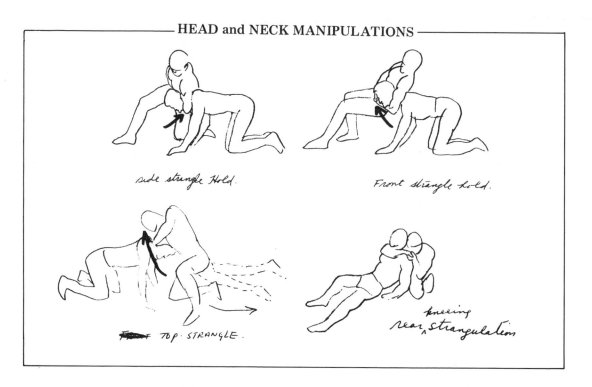

side strangle Hold.

Front strangle hold.

TOP·STRANGLE.

rear strangulation
kneeing

HEAD and ARM MANIPULATIONS

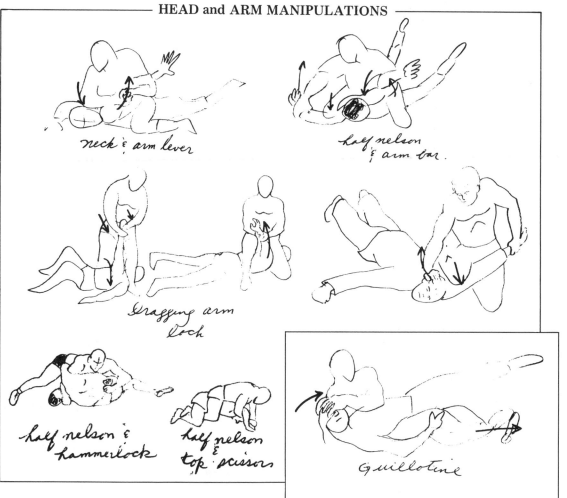

neck & arm lever

half nelson & arm bar.

Dragging arm lock

half nelson & hammerlock

half nelson & top·scissors

Guillotine

Because of the many variables, fighting is a careful game.

武道釋義

All fighting
should be done
with speed and
sudden economy
in mind, as well
as with power.

drop to stomp
or punch to
groin

strangulation to
right stance

strangulation to left stance

watch out for groin
from scarf hold.

straight armlock

stomach throw

Double Armlock (surfboard)

① ② ③

Arm lock

Okuri eri-jime — strangulations

PREPARATIONS

Intelligence is sometimes defined as the capacity of the individual to adjust himself successfully to his environment— or to adjust the environment to his needs.

FEINTS

To minimize the danger of being heavily countered, leads should almost always be preceded by a feint of some sort.

A slight wave of the hand, a stamp of the foot, a sudden shout, etc., can produce *sensory irradiations* sufficient to *reduce coordination*. This mechanism is at the *reflex level* of human behavior and even many years of athletic experience cannot erase the distracting effects of extraneous stimuli.

No feint can be counted effective, however, unless it *forces the opponent to move*. To be successful, it must appear to be a simple movement of attack.

Good feints are *decisive, expressive* and *threatening*, and one can say that JKD is built on feints and the actions connected with them.

The feint is a deceiving thrust which invites and lures the opponent to make the appropriate parry. As the opponent takes the parry, the fighter's hand disengages from the opponent's parrying hand and the thrust is completed in the opened line with either hand. The feint is composed of a *false thrust* and a *real, evasive thrust.*

A slight wave of the hand, a stamp of the foot, a sudden shout . . .

The false thrust is a half-extended arm with a slight forward movement of the upper body. The real, evasive thrust is done with a lunge. *The false thrust must appear so real that it will threaten the opponent into a reaction.* The false thrust must appear to be a real thrust in order to convince the opponent to take the parry.

Feints should be made with the arm more extended (fast! but impress!) if they precede kicking and long-range advancement. If they are made after a parry and the adversary can be reached without a lunge, keep the arm slightly bent and stay well-covered with shifting or a rear guard.

The advantage of a feint or feints is that the attacker can start lunging with his feints and, thus, be *gaining distance* from the outset. He will have shortened the distance to travel by a good half with his feint and left to his second movement only the second half of the disengagement. He *gains distance* by starting his lunge with his feint and, simultaneously, *gains time* by deceiving the parry (the opponent's reaction) on the way to his target.

Feinting is an essential part of attack. The more the opponent can be caught off-guard, or more important still, off-balance by means of feints, the better.

The feint is a deceiving thrust which invites and lures . . .

The speed of your feint is dependent upon the reaction of your opponent. Thus feinting, like speed and distance, must be regulated to your opponent's reaction.

The one-two feints can be utilized laterally (inside/outside; outside/inside) or vertically (high/low; low/high), with only one hand or with the two combined.

The first movement, the feint, must be long and deep, or *penetrating*, to draw the parry. The second movement, the hit, must be fast and decisive in its deception of the parry, allowing the defender no possibility of recovery. Thus, the feint rhythm is *long-short*.

Even in the delivery of compound attacks with two feints, the *depth* of the first feint *must force the opponent to move to the defense*. But, as at this stage the measure has been considerably shortened, the second feint cannot also be long. There is no room and no time to do so. Thus, the rhythm or cadence of a two-feint compound attack will be: *long-short-short*.

A more advanced form of feinting with a *change of cadence* could be described as: *short-long-short*. The object of this variation would be to mislead the adversary, making him believe that the second feint *(long)* was the final action of a compound attack, thus drawing the parry.

By "*long*" we do not really mean slow. While penetrating deeply toward the opponent, the feint must be fast. The combination of speed and penetration are the factors which *draw* the desired reaction from the defense.

If an opponent doesn't react to feints, an attack with straight or simple movements is advisable.

By making several real, *economical*, simple attacks first, the feints will be more effective. The opponent will not know whether a simple attack or a feint followed by a deception is being executed. This is especially effective against the less mobile opponent to promote a reaction. The same tactic might excite the speed-footed opponent into flight.

Feints can also be made in the order of false attacks *to parry the opponent's counter-attack* and riposte or make a fast return or counter-return.

Object of the feint:

1. To open the line in which one intends to attack.
2. To make the opponent hesitate while immediately closing the distance.
3. To deceive the parry which the feint provokes — to trap and hit or to delay the attack and hit as the opponent moves back to recover.

The speed of your feint is dependent upon the reaction of your opponent.

Introduction of the feint:

1. As a direct thrust
2. As an evasive thrust
3. As an engagement
4. As a disengagement
5. As pressure
6. As a violent pressure
7. As a beat
8. As a cut-over (for immobilization)

Parries to evade:

1. Simple
2. Circular
3. Counter or changing

The number of parries to evade can be single, dual or plural.

Execution

Assume the on-guard position. Advance slowly. While advancing, give a quick bend of the forward knee. This gives the impression that the arms are moving as well as legs. In reality, the arms are held relaxed and ready as though committing the lead hand for the opponent.

———————————————————————

Make a slight forward movement of the upper body, bending the forward knee and moving the lead hand slightly forward. While advancing, take a longer step forward with the lead foot, as in the quick advance, and jab the lead arm into extension without hitting the opponent. (Be extra sensitive to counters while advancing—be economical.) From this close position, fold the lead arm back to the body and jab to the chin.

———————————————————————

Another effective feint is a short bend of the body above the rear hip while moving forward.

———————————————————————

The depth of the first feint must force the opponent to move to the defense.

The step-in/step-out feint means stepping forward one step as if to jab with the lead hand, but instead, stepping out of range by pivoting off to the outside with the lead leg. Now, step in as if to feint but drive a lead jab to the chin. Step out immediately. Continue, one time feinting, the next time actually jabbing with the lead hand. If possible, follow the lead jab with a straight rear thrust to the chin (one-two).

———————————————————————

Other feints:

1.   Feint a lead jab to the face and jab to the stomach.

2.   Feint a lead jab to the stomach and jab to the face.

3.   Feint a jab to the face, feint a rear thrust to the face and then jab the lead to the chin.

4.   Feint a straight rear thrust to the jaw and hook the lead to the body.

5.   Feint a lead jab to the chin and deliver a rear uppercut to the body.

Note: Compare all the above for kicking feints. Study head feints explained earlier. Find an accurate feeling for distance and correct balanced posture while feinting.

PARRIES

右擺樁左右手消勢全圖

左擺樁左右手消勢全圖

Find an accurate feeling for distance and correct balanced posture . . .

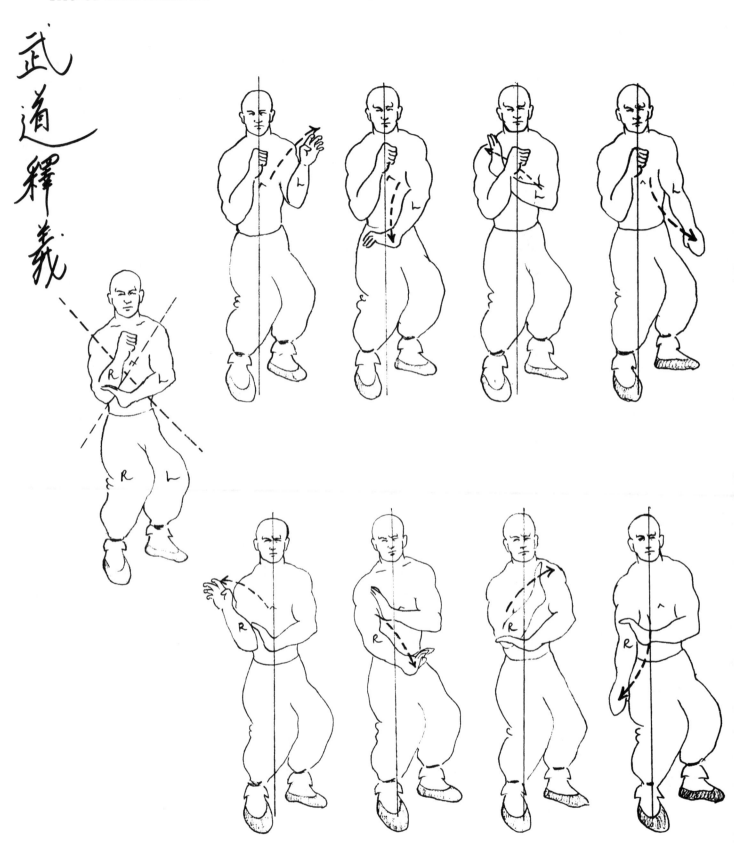

Parrying is a sudden movement of the hand from the inside or outside onto an oncoming blow, to deflect the blow from its original path. It is a *light, easy* movement depending

THE ECONOMY BASE

Parrying is a . . .
***light, easy* movement depending on *timing* . . .**

on *timing* rather than force. A blow is never parried until the last moment and always when close to the body.

There are three parries — simple, semicircular, circular — to a single offensive movement.

If the attacker's movements are large and badly directed, a *simple parry* would be the answer. (Don't forget the stop-hit.) Simple parries tend to be used without discrimination because they are instinctive movements. Thus, great care must be taken that they are well-controlled and cover just enough. Avoid any slashing or whipping of the guards. (Remember simplicity. Study the eight basic defensive positions.)

The object in the parry is to use just enough deflecting motion to protect the threatened area. If you over-protect (move the hand too far to one side), you are immediately vulnerable to disengaging attacks.

To reach out to parry a blow not only makes openings for counter-blows, but also enables the opponent to change the direction of his blow. Remember, *parry late rather than early.*

Parrying is an extremely useful form of defense. It is easily learned, easily performed and should be used whenever possible. *Advantageous openings are created which are essential to counter-fighting.*

———————————

Parrying is more refined than blocking which uses force and causes contusion of the tissues, nerves and bones. Blocking should be used only when it is necessary because it weakens rather than conserves bodily force. A well-delivered blow, even if blocked, will disturb balance, prevent countering and create openings for other blows.

———————————

Successful parries are brought about by placing the defensive hand across the path of the thrust so that should there be any force in the blow, it would slide off.

———————————

Sometimes the fighter must feel that in deflecting the thrust or kick, he is in reality taking possession of it; that through the contact he obtains, he will feel his opponent's reactions when the latter realizes his attack has failed.

———————————

Only use a parry against a real attack. The opponent's false attacks can be followed with half positions.

Sweep away the thrust from the target by the shortest route.

———————————

Exercises: The teacher directs strikes or thrusts to different parts of the target. The student follows these movements but stops when the teacher stops, parrying only the real attacks. Next, the teacher makes the same threats, but the student does not follow with his hand. Again, the parry is taken only when the real strike or thrust comes. This procedure teaches the student to parry only at the last moment.

———————————

Against the simple parry (that is, a lateral crossing of hands) attack with disengagement (on another line).

———————————

When making the opposition parry to apply the *"beat"* parry, your hand should not swing too far to the right or left. Merely close the line or deflect the opponent's hand, leaving just enough room to arrive on the target.

———————————

The beat parry is usually followed by a fast return against the sharp and powerful opponent.

———————————

Semicircular parries are those taken from a high line of engagement to deflect an attack

directed in the low line, or from a low line engagement to a high line. They describe a half-circle.

The parries of octave (low outside) and septime (low inside) are those used for defense against attacks directed in the low line, but for tactical reasons they can be alternatives to the parries of sixte (high outside) and quarte (high inside). *Study the parries in fencing.*

Against a very fast fighter or one with a marked superiority of height or reach, it is often necessary to step backwards when making a parry. When parrying with a step backwards, the parry should be taken as the rear foot moves backwards in the course of breaking ground. In other words, the parry should be formed *with* the step back and not after it has been completed.

A circular parry envelops the attacker's wrist and brings it back to the original line of invitation, while deflecting it off the target.

The step back as a defensive movement should always be *adjusted* to the length of the opponent's attacking movements to ensure that the required measure is maintained for a successful parry and riposte.

A *circular parry* envelops the attacker's wrist and brings it back to the original line of invitation, while deflecting it off the target.

Sweep away the thrust from the target by the shortest route (with your shoulder relaxed) — counter of sixte is taken by moving the hand clockwise, while counter of quarte will require a counterclockwise rotation of the blade.

A circular parry, when used in the high line, starts under the adversary's hand; when used in the low line, it starts over the opponent's hand. The advantages of circular parries over opposition or beat parries is that they protect a larger amount of the target and are more difficult to deceive. However, they are not as rapid as the simple parries. Time spent in speeding them up will pay good dividends.

When using the circular parries, be sure that the hand describes a perfect circle so that it finishes in its original position. Do not start or finish the parry too soon, for your hand *must follow the opponent's* and should meet his hand just before it is about to arrive on the target.

Use the circular parry also to mess up the opponent who feints.

Compound parries consist of two or more like parries or a combination of different parries.

Each single parry *must be finished*, bringing your hand to the "appropriate" position, before making the succeeding parry.

Mix and vary your parries so the opponent cannot set an attacking plan. The habit of always reacting to attacks with the same type of parry will obviously play into the hands of an observant opponent. Thus, it is wise to vary the type of parry used as much as possible during a bout to keep the opponent guessing. This will cause a certain amount of hesitation on the part of the attacker whose offensive action will suffer in confidence and penetration.

Mix and vary your parries so the opponent cannot set an attacking plan.

What will make parries or blocks more effective? — body positioning, footwork (moving in, circling, etc.) to facilitate ready countering.

Watch out for the opponent's counter.

Experiment *sweeping* the parry *toward the opponent's path* (natural easy movements).

Examine parries with all kinds of dodging, shifting, slipping, weaving, ducking, snapping back, for possible insertion of kicks or a combination of kicks and/or punches. Insert stopping and covering with kick and punch insertions. Also, be sure to constantly threaten the opponent with inserts during apparent shifts to various directions (commitments) so as to always be positioning *on-guard*.

MANIPULATIONS

THE BEAT

If the opponent is exceptionally fast and will not go for feints, the beat can be used.

The beat is a crisp movement of the hand made against the opponent's with the object of knocking it aside or obtaining a reaction. Usually the reaction of the fighter to beat back will offer the advantage of staying ahead of the opponent's movement throughout.

Because of the distance, the beat cannot be made at will. The correct opportunity must be waited for and seized. The opponent's continual change of hand position, often in the form of half-feints and false attacks, will bring the hand well within reach of a beat.

Although a beat followed by a direct attack can be successful, beats generally bring about a covering movement to the side on which the hand has been beaten. This makes a direct attack a difficult stroke to bring off. It is advisable, therefore, to take advantage of such reactions by following the beat with an indirect or compound attack. The beat should be made from the normal guard position into the line in which the hands are engaged. If a change of engagement is made to beat on another line, the action is called a *change beat*.

The correct opportunity must be waited for and seized.

Make the beat sharp and as close to the hand as possible. There are three purposes to making beats on the hand:

1. To open the line by force or, by the right amount of crispiness on the opponent's "tension spring," to secure thread-like penetration.

2. As a feint before an attack.

3. As an invitation to the opponent's attack, especially after obtaining his cadence.

In the first case, the beat on the hand should be made *sharply* and *quickly*; practice trapping or hand immobilization with these two qualities along with the small phasic bent-knee stance.

In the second case, the beat should be light and fast so as to pass the hand quickly and execute the attack.

In the third case, it should be made lightly and not too quickly, at the same time being ready to either parry the attack, counter-time it or follow with a second light and fast beat to counterattack.

THE BIND

When the hand is engaged, the action of carrying the opponent's hand *diagonally across* from a high to a low line or vice versa is called a "bind." It is performed much like a semicircular parry.

THE CROISE

The croise carries the opponent's hand from the high to low line *on the same side* of the engagement and does not, as in the bind, carry it diagonally across. It is *not* executed from low to high.

THE ENVELOPMENT

The envelopment is the action of taking the opponent's hand off its target in a circular motion and returning it to the line of engagement.

The bind, croise, envelopment and pressure are mainly elements of trapping prior to an indirect attack or are simply used to obtain a reaction.

THE PRESSURE

The pressure is the action of pressing upon the opponent's hand in order to deflect it or obtain a reaction to disengage from it.

The beat is used prior to a direct attack or to obtain a reaction for an indirect attack. The bind, croise, envelopment and pressure are mainly elements of trapping prior to an indirect attack or are simply used to obtain a reaction.

MOBILITY

Attain stillness while moving, like thy moon beneath the waves that ever go on rolling and rocking.

DISTANCE

Distance is a continually shifting relationship, depending on the speed, agility and control of both fighters. It is a constant, rapid shifting of ground, seeking the slightest closing which will greatly increase the chances of hitting the opponent.

———————————————

The maintenance of proper fighting distance has a decisive effect on the outcome of the fight—acquire the habit!

———————————————

There must be close synchronization between closing and opening distance and the various actions of the hands and feet. To fight for any length of time within distance is safe only if you overwhelmingly outclass your opponent in speed and agility.

———————————————

When taking the guard, it is preferable to fall back a little too far than to come too close to your opponent. No matter how fast you are able to parry, if a man is close enough to you he will arrive with his attack, for the nature of an attack is such that it gives the advantage of the initiation to the attacker (providing the correct measure is there). Likewise, however accurate, fast, economical and timely your attack may be, it will fall short unless you have calculated your distance well.

There must be close synchronization between closing and opening distance.

———————————————

The *fighting measure* is the distance which a fighter keeps in relation to his opponent. It is such that he cannot be hit unless his opponent lunges fully at him.

———————————————

It is essential that each man learn his own fighting measure. This means in a fight he must allow for the relative agility and speed of himself and his opponent. That is, he should *consistently stay out of distance* in the sense that his opponent cannot reach him with a simple punch, but not so far that, *with a short advance*, he cannot regain the distance and be able to reach his opponent with his own powerful attack.

———————————————

If fighters are constantly on the move when fighting, it is because they are trying to make their opponent misjudge his distance while being well aware of their own.

———————————————

Thus, a fighter is constantly gaining and breaking ground in his effort to obtain the distance which suits him best. Develop the *reflex* of always maintaining a correct measure. Instinctive distance pacing is of utmost importance.

The shielded fighter always keeps himself just out of distance of the opponent's attack and waits for his opportunity to close the distance himself or to *steal a march* on the opponent's advance. Attack *on the opponent's advance* or change of distance toward you. Back him to a wall to cut off his retreat or retreat yourself to *draw* an advance.

The majority of *fencers*, when they are preparing an attack or trying to avoid one, take turns advancing and retreating. This procedure is not advisable in fighting because the advance and retreat during the assault must be made rapidly, by bounds and at irregular intervals in such a fashion that the adversary does not notice the action until it is too late. The opponent should be lulled, then the attack should be launched as suddenly as possible, accommodating itself to the automatic movements (including the possible retreat) of the opponent.

The art of successful kicking and hitting is the art of correct distance judging. An attack should be aimed at the distance where the opponent *will be* when he realizes he is being attacked and not at the distance prior to the attack. The slightest error can render the attack harmless.

It is essential that each man learn his own fighting measure.

An attack will rarely succeed unless you can lodge yourself at the correct distance *at the moment it is launched*. A parry is most likely to succeed if it can be made just as the opponent is at the end of his lunge. Many a chance to riposte is missed by the defender stepping back completely out of distance when he parries. To these examples must be added the obvious importance of choosing the correct measure, as well as *timing and cadence*, when making a counterattack by stop-hit or time-hit.

Marcelli, past master of fencing, said, "The question whether it is necessary to know in advance the tempo or the distance is a matter for the philosopher rather than the swordsman to decide. Just the same, it is certain that the combatant has to observe simultaneously both the tempo and the distance. And he has to comply with both *simultaneously*, with the action, if he wishes to reach his object."

The fighting measure is also governed by the amount of target to be protected (i.e.: the targets the adversary stresses) and the parts of the body which are most easily within the adversary's reach. The shin is most vulnerable and is constantly threatened. If the opponent specializes in shin/knee kicking, you have to take his measure from shin to shin.

When the correct distance is attained, the attack should be carried through with an instantaneous burst of energy and speed. A fighter who is in a constant state of physical fitness is more apt to get off the mark in a fraction of a second and, therefore, to seize an opportunity without warning.

DISTANCE IN ATTACK

The first principle for fastest contact in attacking from a distance is using the longest to get at the closest.

Examples   In kicking: The leading shin/knee side kick (with a lean)
               In striking: The finger jab to eyes

Study the progressive weapons charts.

The second principle is economical initiation (non-telegraphic). Apply latent motor training to intuition.

The third principle is correct on-guard position to facilitate freedom of movement (ease). Use the small phasic bent-knee position.

The fourth principle is constant shifting of footwork to secure the correct measure. Use broken rhythm to confuse the opponent's distance while controlling one's own.

The slightest error can render the attack harmless.

The fifth principle is catching the opponent's moment of weakness, physically as well as psychologically.

The sixth principle is correct measure for explosive penetration.

The seventh principle is quick recovery or appropriate follow-ups.

The "X" principle is courage and decision.

DISTANCE IN DEFENSE

The first principle for using distance as a defense is combining sensitive *aura* with co-ordinated footwork.

The second principle is good judgment of the opponent's length of penetration, a sense for receiving his straightening weapon to borrow the half-beat.

The third principle is correct on-guard position to facilitate freedom of movement (ease). Use small phasic bent-knee position.

The fourth principle is the use of controlled balance (in motion) without moving out of position. Study evasiveness.

FOOTWORK

One can only develop an instinctive sense of distance if he is able to move about smoothly and speedily.

When the correct distance is attained, the attack should be carried through...

The quality of a man's technique depends on his footwork, for one cannot use his hands or kicks efficiently until his feet have put him in the desired position. If a man is slow on his feet, he will be slow with his punches and kicks. Mobility and speed of footwork precede speed of kicks and punches.

Mobility is definitely stressed in Jeet Kune Do because combat is a matter of motion, an operation of finding a target or of avoiding being a target. In this art, there is no nonsense of squatting on a classical horse stance for three long years before moving. This type of unnecessary, strenuous standing is not functional, for it is basically a seeking of firmness in stillness. *In Jeet Kune Do, one finds firmness in movement, which is real, easy and alive.* Therefore, springiness and alertness of footwork is the theme.

During sparring, a sparmate is constantly on the move to make his opponent misjudge his distance, while being quite certain of his own. In fact, the length of the step forward and backward is regulated to that of his opponent. A good man always maintains such a position as to enable him, while keeping just out of range, to be yet near enough to immediately take an opening (ref.: the fighting measure). Thus, at a normal distance, he is able to prevent his opponent from attacking him by his fine sense of distance and timing. As a result, his opponent is then compelled to keep shortening his distance, to come nearer and nearer until he is too near!

Mobility is vitally important in defense as well, for a moving target is definitely harder to hit and kick. Footwork can and will beat any kick or punch. The more adept a fighter is at footwork, the less does he make use of his arms in avoiding kicks and blows. By means of skillful and timely sidestepping and slipping, he can get clear of almost any kick and punch, thus preserving both of his guns, as well as his balance and energy, for counters.

―――――――――

Also, by constantly being in small motion, the fighter can initiate a movement much more snappily than from a position. It is not recommended, therefore, that you stay too long on the same spot. Always use short steps to alter the distance between you and your opponent. Vary the length of your step, however, as well as the speed, for added confusion to your opponent.

―――――――――

Footwork in Jeet Kune Do tends to aim toward simplification with a minimum of movement. *Do not get carried away and stand on your toes and dance all over the place like a fancy boxer.* Economical footwork not only adds speed but, by moving just enough to evade the opponent's attack, it commits him fully. The simple idea is to get where you are safe and he isn't.

―――――――――

Above all, footwork should be easy and relaxing. The feet are kept at a comfortable distance apart according to the individual, without any strain or awkwardness. By now the reader should see the unrealistic approach of the traditional, classical footwork and stances. They are slow and awkward and, to put it plainly, nobody moves like that in a fight! A martial artist is required to shift in any direction at split second notice.

The quality of a man's technique depends on his footwork. . .

―――――――――

Moving is used as a means of defense, a means of deception, a means of securing proper distance for attack and a means of conserving energy. *The essence of fighting is the art of moving.*

―――――――――

Footwork enables you to break ground and escape punishment, to get out of a tight corner, to allow the heavy slugger to tire himself in his vain attempts to land a devastating punch; it also puts pep into the punch.

―――――――――

The greatest phase of footwork is the coordination of punching and kicking in motion. Without footwork, the fighter is like artillery that cannot be moved or a policeman in the wrong place at the wrong time.

―――――――――

The value of a couple of good hands and fast, powerful kicking depends mostly on

their being on a well-balanced and quickly movable base. It is essential, therefore, to preserve the balance and poise of the fighting turret carrying your artillery. No matter in what direction or at what speed you move, your aim is to *retain the fundamental stance* which has been found the most effective for fighting. Let the movable pedestal be as nimble as possible.

The correct style in fighting is that which, in its absolute naturalness, combines velocity and power of hitting with the soundest defense.

Good footwork means good balance in action and from this springs hitting power and the ability to avoid punishment. Every movement involves the coordination of hands, feet and brain.

A fighter should not be flatfooted but should *feel* the floor with the balls of his feet as though they were strong springs, ready to accelerate or retard his movements as required by changing conditions.

In Jeet Kune Do, one finds firmness in movement, which is real, easy and alive.

Use the feet cleverly to maneuver and combine balanced movement with aggression and protection. Above all, keep cool.

    \#   The foundation is sensitivity of aura.

    \#   The second is aliveness and naturalness.

    \#   The third is instinctive pacing (distance and timing).

    \#   The fourth is correct placement of the body.

    \#   The fifth is a balanced position at the end.

Use your own footwork and your opponent's to your advantage. Note his pattern, if any, of advancing and retreating. Vary the length and speed of your own step.

The length of the step forward or backward should be approximately regulated to that of the opponent.

Variations of measure will make it more difficult for the opponent to time his attacks or preparations. A fighter with a good sense of distance or one who is difficult to reach in launching an attack may often be brought to the desired measure by progressively shortening a series of steps backward or by gaining distance toward him when he lunges (stealing the march).

The simplest and most fundamental tactic to use on an opponent is to gain just enough distance to facilitate a hit. The idea is to press (advance) a step or so and then fall back (retreat), inviting the opponent to follow. Allow your opponent to advance a step or two and then, *at the precise moment he lifts his foot for still another step*, you must suddenly lunge forward into his step.

An opponent difficult to reach may be reached by a series of progressive steps — the first one must be smooth and economical.

Small and rapid steps are recommended as the only way to keep perfect balance, exact distance and the ability to apply sudden attacks or counterattacks.

Sure footwork and balance are necessary to be able to advance and retreat in and out of distance with respect to both your own and your opponent's reach. Knowing when to advance and when to retreat is also knowing when to attack and when to protect.

A good man steals, creates and changes the vital spatial relations to the confusion of his opponent.

Footwork in Jeet Kune Do tends to aim toward simplification.

Practice your footwork with a view to keeping a very correct and precise distance in relation to your opponent and move just enough to accomplish your purpose. Fine distancing will make the opponent strive that much harder, and thus bring him close enough to be subject to efficient counterblows.

To move at the right time is the foundation of great skill in fighting, not *just* to move at the right time but also to be in the best position for attack or counter. It means balance, but *balance in movement*.

Having your feet in the correct position serves as a pivot for your entire attack. It balances you properly and lends unseen power to your blows, just as it does in sports like baseball where drive and power seem to come up from the legs.

To maintain balance while constantly shifting body weight is an art few ever acquire.

Correct placement of your feet will ensure balance and mobility — experiment with

yourself. You must *feel* with your footwork. Rapid and easy footwork is a matter of correct distribution of weight.

The ideal position of the feet is one that enables you to move quickly in any direction and to be so balanced as to resist blows from all angles. *Remember the small phasic bent-knee stance.*

The essence of fighting is the art of moving.

The rear heel is raised because:
1. When you punch, you transfer all your weight quickly to your lead leg. This is easier if the rear heel is already slightly raised.
2. When you are punched and have to "give" a bit, you sink down on the rear heel. This acts as a kind of spring and takes the edge out of a punch.
3. It makes the back foot easier to move.

The rear heel is the piston of the whole fighting machine.

The feet must always be directly under the body. Any movement of the feet which tends to unbalance the body *must be eliminated.* The on-guard position is one of perfect body balance and should always be maintained, especially as regards the feet. *Wide steps or leg movements which require a constant shift of weight from one leg to the other cannot be used.* During this shift of weight, there is a moment when balance is precarious and so renders attack or defense ineffective. Also, the opponent can time your shifting for his attack.

Short steps while moving ensure balance in attack. Also, the body balance is always maintained so that any offensive or defensive movement required is not limited or impaired as the fighter moves forward, backward or circles his opponent. Thus, it is better to take two medium steps rather than one long one to cover the same distance.

Variations of measure will make it more difficult for the opponent to time his attacks or preparation.

Unless there is a tactical reason for acting otherwise, gaining and breaking ground is executed by means of *small* and *rapid steps*. A correct distribution of weight on both legs will make for perfect balance, enabling the fighter to get off the mark quickly and easily whenever the measure is right for attacks.

Lighten the stance so the force of inertia to be overcome will be less. The best way to learn proper footwork is to shadow box many rounds, giving special attention to becoming light on your feet. Gradually, this way of stepping around will become natural to you and you will do it easily and mechanically without giving it a thought.

Every movement involves the co-ordination of hands, feet and brain.

You should operate in the same manner as a graceful ballroom dancer who uses the feet, ankles and calves. He slithers around the floor.

The accent is on speedy footwork and the tendency toward attack with a step forward (drill! drill! drill!), often combined with an attack *on the hand.*

There are only four moves possible in footwork:
1. Advancing
2. Retreating
3. Circling right
4. Circling left

However, there are important variations of each, as well as the necessity of coordinating each fundamental movement with punches and kicks. The following are some examples:

The forward shuffle: This is a forward advance of the body, without disturbing body balance, which can only be performed through a series of short steps forward. These steps must be so small that the feet are not lifted at all, but slide along the floor. The whole body maintains the fundamental position throughout; this is the key. Once *body feel* results, combine the step with tools. The body is poised for either sudden attack or a defensive maneuver. Its primary purpose is to create openings (by the opponent's defensive reactions) and to draw leads.

The backward shuffle: The principle is the same as that of the forward shuffle; do it without disturbing the on-guard position. Remember that both feet are on the floor *at all times*, permitting balance to be maintained for attack or defense. It is used to draw leads or to draw the opponent off-balance, thus creating openings.

The quick advance: Remember that though this is a fast, sudden movement forward, balance must be kept. The body *flattens toward the floor* rather than leaping into the air. *It is not a hop.* In all respects, it is the same as a wide step forward where the rear foot is brought immediately into position. *Get the body feel* with tools.

Lighten the stance so the force of inertia to be overcome will be less.

The step forward and the step back: Gaining and breaking ground may be used *as a preparation of attack*. The step forward is obviously used to *obtain the correct distance for attacking* and the step back can be used to *draw the opponent within distance*. "Drawing" an opponent usually means drawing out of distance from a lead by swaying back from the hips, or making use of the feet in such a way that the lead will just fall short. Its object is to lure your opponent within reach at a crucial moment, while staying out of reach yourself.

The step forward will add speed to the attack when it is combined with a feint (forcing the opponent to commit himself) *or a preparation* (to tie and close the boundaries). If the step forward is made with the line of engagement covered, the attacker will be in the best position to deal with a stop-hit launched during this movement.

The step back can be used tactically against an opponent who has formed the habit of retiring whenever any feint or other offensive movement is made and is, therefore, very difficult to reach, especially if he is superior in height and length.

Constant steps forward and back with a carefully regulated length can *conceal a player's intentions* and enable him to lodge himself at the ideal distance for an attack, often as the opponent is off-balance.

Circling right: The right lead leg becomes a movable pivot that wheels the whole body to the right until the correct position is resumed. The first step with the right foot may be as short or as long as necessary — the longer the step, the greater the pivot. The fundamental position must be maintained *at all times*. The right hand should be carried a little higher than ordinary in readiness for the opponent's left counter. Moving to the right may be used to nullify an opponent's right lead hook. It may be used to get into position for left hand counters and it can be used to keep the opponent off-balance. The important things to remember are never step so as to cross the feet, move deliberately and without excess motion.

Circling left: This is a more precise movement requiring shorter steps. It is used to keep out of range of rear, left hand blows from a right stancer. It also creates good position for the delivery of a hook or jab. It is more difficult but safer than moving to the right and, therefore, should be used more often.

The step-in/step-out: This is the start of an offensive maneuver, often used as a feint in order to build up an opening. The foot movement is always combined with kicking and punching movement. The initial movement (the step-in) is directly in, with the hands held high as if to hit or kick, then out quickly before the opponent can adjust his defense. Lull the opponent with this maneuver, then attack when he is motorset.

It is a continuous process of hit-and-away.

The quick retreat: This is a fast, fluid, forceful backward movement, allowing further retreat if necessary or a stepping forward to attack if desired.

If it is necessary to combine a step back with a parry, it is because one is pressed for time. The parry must, therefore, be made at the *beginning* of the retreating movement — that is to say, *when the rear foot moves*.

When the opponent's offensive action is a compound one, the correct coordination will be to perform the first parry simultaneously with the movement of the rear foot, and the remaining parry, or parries, simultaneously with the retreating lead foot.

The step back can be taken first, but this should only be the case when the attack has been *prepared* with a step forward and not when the attack has been *made* with a step forward.

To a man with quick footwork and a good lead, the art comes easily enough. It is a continuous process of hit-and-away. As your opponent moves in, you meet him with

a defensive hit with the lead and immediately step back; then, as he follows-up, you repeat the process, continually retreating *around the ring*. As you do so, frequently check yourself in your stride and temporarily stop to meet him with a straight right or left or occasionally both.

Success in "milling on the retreat" takes good judgment of distance and the ability to stop in your retreat quickly and unexpectedly. The common fault is to deliver your blow while actually on the move instead of properly stopping to do it. Develop great rapidity in passing from defense to attack and then back to defense again.

Remember, do not attempt to hit while backing away. Your weight has to shift forward. Step back, halt, then hit or learn to shift your body weight momentarily forward while the foot backs up.

Whether on the offensive or retreating, one should strive to be a confusing and difficult target. One should not move in a straight forward or in a straight backward direction.

The turret carrying the artillery must remain well-poised, a constant threat to your foe.

When avoiding or maneuvering your opponent by footwork, keep as near to him as you can for retaliatory purposes. Move lightly, feeling the floor as a springboard, ready to snap in with a punch, kick or a counterpunch or kick.

To retreat from *kicks* is to give the adversary room so it is wise, at times, to crowd and smother his preparation and gain time consequently with a stop-hit.

Sidestepping: Sidestepping is actually shifting the weight and changing the feet without disturbing balance in an effort to quickly gain a more advantageous position from which to carry the attack. It is used to avoid straight forward rushes and to move quickly out of range. When an opponent rushes you, it is not so much the rush you sidestep as *some particular blow* he leads during the rush.

Sidestepping is a safe, sure and valuable defensive tactic. You can use it to frustrate an attack simply by moving every time an opponent gets set to attack or you may use it as a method of avoiding blows or kicks. It may also be used to create openings for a counterattack.

Sidestepping may be performed by shifting the body forward, which is called a *"forward drop."* This is a pretty safe position with the head in close, the hands carried high and ready to strike the opponent's groin, or stomp on his insteps, or carry a two-fisted hooking attack. The forward drop, also called a *"drop shift,"* is used to gain either the outside or inside guard position and is, therefore, a very useful technique in in-fighting or grappling. It is also a vehicle for countering. It requires timing, speed and judgment to properly execute and may be combined with the jab, straight left, left and right hooks.

The same step may also be performed *directly* to the right or left or back, depending on the degree of safety needed or the plan of action.

Properly used, sidestepping is not only one of the prettiest moves, but is also a method of escaping all kinds of attacks and countering an opponent when he least expects it. The art of sidestepping, as of ducking and slipping, is to *move late and quick.* You wait until your opponent's kick or blow is almost on you and then take a quick step either to the right or left.

In nearly all cases, you move first the foot nearest the direction you intend to go in. In order to do the step in the quickest possible manner, the body should sway over in the direction you are going slightly before the step is made. The rear foot then follows quickly and naturally and, in sidestepping a rush, the fighter turns immediately and counters his man as he flies past him.

When an opponent rushes you, it is not so much the rush you sidestep as some particular blow he leads during the rush.

When sidestepping a lead, the counter is naturally quite easy. Not so after a rush for to counter effectively here, a fighter has to keep very close to his opponent, moving just enough to make him miss. The fighter must then turn extraordinarily quickly to be on him before he has flashed past.

Remember, when an opponent rushes you, it is not so much the rush you sidestep as some particular kick or blow he leads during the rush; indeed, if you step to the side of your opponent without catching sight of some blow to get outside of, you will be very liable to run into a hook or a swing.

Sidestepping right: Carry the right lead foot sharply to the right and forward, a distance of about 18 inches. Bring up the left foot an equal distance behind the right. The step serves to swing the body to the left, bringing the right side farther forward and closer to the opponent's left rear (when in a right stance himself). For that reason, the right sidestep is not used as frequently as the one to the left. Most of the weaving and sidestepping is to the left, keeping you closer to his right and farther away from his left rear hand. (The situation changes in right-stancer versus left-stancer.)

Occasionally, a right sidestep is taken just to vary the direction of the weaving and, even less frequently in, slipping a right lead, getting inside of it to counter with a left. It is used in starting a left to the body.

———————

Sidestepping left: From the fundamental right stance position, bring the left foot sharply to the left and forward a distance of about 18 inches. This should carry you to the *outside* of the opponent's right jab. You will find just as you take the step to the left, the left side of your body swings forward and the right side back, so that you *rotate toward the opponent's right flank.* As you complete this half-circle movement, you will find that your right foot is again in its normal position ahead of the left foot.

———————

If you have taken the sidestep to the left to avoid the opponent's right lead, you should sway your body and duck your head (without losing balance) in the direction of the step — that is to the left. His right will swish by, over your head, in the direction of your right shoulder. Now, as you wheel to the right toward the opponent, you have his whole right flank exposed and can quickly land a left to the body or jaw with telling effect.

Aim always to move fluidly but retain the relative position of the two feet.

Remember this simple thought: Move first the foot closest to the direction you wish to go in. In other words, if you wish to sidestep to the left, move the left foot first and vice versa. Also, in all *hand* techniques, the hand moves first, *before* the foot. When foot techniques are used, of course, move the foot first, before the hand.

———————

Remember also to always retain the fundamental stance. No matter what you do with that moving pedestal, the turret carrying the artillery must remain well-poised, a constant threat to your foe. Aim always to move fluidly but retain the relative position of the two feet.

———————

Examine footwork for:
1. Body feel and control, as a whole, in neutralness.
2. Attack and defense capability at all times.
3. Ease and comfort in every direction.

4.   Application of efficient leverage during all phases of movement.
5.   Superb balancing at all times.
6.   Elusiveness in well-protected corresponding structure and correct distancing.

Experiment on the following *mechanics* and *feeling* of footwork:
1.   Footwork to be evasive and soft if the opponent is rushing.
2.   Footwork to avoid contact point (as if the opponent is armed with a knife.)

The ultimate aim is still to obtain the *brim of the fire-line* on the opponent's final real thrusts.

Remember, *mobility* and *rapidity* of footwork and *speed of execution* are primary qualities. Practice footwork and more footwork.

Footwork can be gained also by skipping rope (an exercise to learn how to handle one's body weight lightly), sparring (the learning of distance and timing in footwork) and shadow kickboxing (homework for sparring).

Running will also strengthen the legs to supply boundless energy for efficient operation.

> Mobility and rapidity of footwork and speed of execution are primary qualities.

Increase control of the legs through medium squatting posture exercises and ape-imitation movement (low walking).

Incorporate alternate leg splits for flexibility.

No matter how simple the strokes being practiced in the lesson are or whether they are of an offensive or defensive nature, the practitioner must be made to combine footwork with them. He must be made to advance or retire *before*, *while* and *after* the stroke he is working on has been executed. In this way, he will acquire a natural sense of distance and develop great mobility.

Practice footwork variations along with
1.   kicking tools
2.   hand tools
3.   covered hand and/or knee positions

EVASIVENESS

During fighting, there is a good deal of parrying, especially with the rear hand, but it is better to use footwork — duck and counter, snap back and return, slip and punch.

SLIPPING

Slipping is avoiding a blow without actually moving the body out of range. It is used *primarily* against straight leads and counters. It calls for exact timing and judgment and, to be effective, it must be executed so that the blow is escaped only by the smallest fraction.

Slipping is avoiding a blow without actually moving the body out of range.

It is possible to slip either a left or a right lead. Actually, slipping is more often used on the forward hand lead because it is safer. The outside slip, that is, dropping to a position outside the opponent's left or right lead, is safest and leaves the opponent unable to defend against a counterattack.

Slipping is a most valuable technique, leaving both hands free to counter. It is the real basis of counter-fighting and is performed by the expert.

Slipping inside a left lead — As the opponent leads a straight left, drop your weight back to your rear left leg by quickly turning your right shoulder and body to the left.

(opponent in left stance)
連環綿沖

Your left foot remains stationary but your right shoulder pivots inward. This movement allows his left hand to slip over your right shoulder as you obtain the inside guard position.

Slipping outside a left lead — As the opponent leads a straight left, shift your weight right and forward over your right leg, swinging your left shoulder forward. The blow will slip over your left shoulder. A short step forward and to the right with your right foot facilitates the movement. Your hands should be carried high in a guard position.

Slipping is the real basis of counter-fighting and is performed by the expert.

(opponent in right stance)
連環綿沖

Slipping inside a right lead — As the opponent leads a right punch, shift your weight over your lead right leg, thus moving your body slightly to the right and forward. Bring your left shoulder quickly forward. In doing so, the punch will slip over your left shoulder. Be sure to rotate your left hip inward and bend your left knee slightly. The inside position is the preferred position for attack. Move your head separately *only* if the slip is too narrow.

Slipping outside a right lead — As the opponent leads a right, drop your weight back on your left leg and quickly turn your right shoulder and body to the right. Your right foot remains stationary and your left toe pivots inward. The punch will slip harmlessly by. Drop your right hand slightly, but hold it ready to drive an uppercut

to the opponent's body. Your left hand should be held high, near your right shoulder, ready to counter to his chin.

——————————————

Another method is to shift your weight to your left leg and pivot your right heel outward so that your right shoulder and your body turn to the left. Drop your right hand slightly and keep your left hand high, near your right shoulder.

——————————————

When slipping, the shoulder roll will shift your head — don't tilt it unnaturally.

——————————————

Try to always hit on the slip, particularly when moving forward. You can hit harder when stepping inside a punch than when you block and counter or parry and counter.

——————————————

The key to successful slipping often lies in a little movement of the heel. For example, if it is desired to slip a lead to the right so that it passes over your left shoulder, your left heel should be lifted and twisted outwards. Transferring your weight to your right foot and twisting your shoulders will set you up nicely to counter.

——————————————

It is just as necessary to learn to duck swings and hooks as it is to slip straight punches.

To slip a lead over your right shoulder with a defensive movement to the left, your right heel should be twisted in similar fashion. Your weight is thus shifted to your left foot and your left shoulder is to the rear, so you are favorably placed to counter with a right hook.

——————————————

If you remember that the shoulder over which you desire to slip a blow and the heel to be twisted are one and the same, you will not go far wrong. Exceptions are movements similar to the first description of "slipping outside a right lead."

——————————————

DUCKING

Ducking is dropping the body forward under swings and hooks (hands or feet) directed at the head. It is executed primarily from the waist. Ducking is used as a means of escaping blows and allowing the fighter to remain in range for a counterattack. It is just as necessary to learn to duck swings and hooks as it is to slip straight punches. Both are important in counterattacks.

——————————————

THE SNAP BACK

The snap back means simply to snap the body away from a straight lead enough to make the opponent miss. As the opponent's arm relaxes to his body, it is possible to move in with a stiff counter. This is a very effective technique against a lead jab and may also be used as the basis of the one-two combination blow.

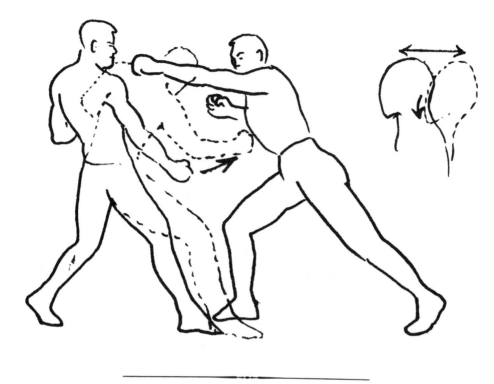

ROLLING

Rolling nullifies the force of a blow by moving the body with it.
    # Against a straight blow, the movement is *backward.*
    # Against hooks, the movement is *to either side.*
    # Against uppercuts, it is *backward and away.*
    # Against hammers, it is a *circular movement down to either side.*

The fundamental asset of the clever fighter is the sliding roll.

THE SLIDING ROLL

The fundamental asset of the clever fighter is the sliding roll. He spots the punch or a high kick coming, perhaps instinctively, and takes one step back, sweeping his head back and underneath. He is now in a position to come up with several handy blows or kicks into nice openings.

THE BODY SWAY
(bob and weave)

The art of swaying renders the fighter more difficult to hit and gives him more power, particularly with the hook. It is useful in that it leaves the hands open for attack, improving the defense and providing opportunities to hit hard when openings occur.

The key to swaying is relaxation and the stiff, rigid type of boxer must be easier to deal with than the ever-swaying type.

Mechanics of the bob:

1. Sink under the swing or hook with a single, perfectly controlled movement.
2. Bring your fists in toward your opponent for guarding or attacking.
3. Maintain a nearly normal punching position with your legs and feet, even at the bottom of the bob. Use your knees to provide the motion.
4. Maintain at all times the normal slipping position of your head and shoulders for defense against straight punches. It is extremely important that you be in position to slip at any stage of the bob.
5. Don't counter on a straight-down bob except, perhaps, with a straight thrust to the groin. Weave to apply delayed counters with whirling straight punches or hooks.

Weaving is used to make an opponent miss and to sustain a counterattack with both hands.

Purposes of the weave:

1. To make a moving target of your head (from side to side).
2. To make your opponent uncertain about which way you will slip if he punches at you.
3. To make your opponent uncertain about which fist you will throw when you punch.

Weaving means moving the body in, out and around a straight lead to the head. It is used to make an opponent miss and to sustain a counterattack with both hands. Weaving is based on slipping and is a circular movement of the upper trunk and head, right or left.

a)   b)

Weaving to the inside — On a right lead, slip to the outside position (figure A). Drop your head and upper body, move in under the extended right lead and then up to the basic position. The opponent's right lead now approximates your left shoulder (figure B). Carry your hands high and close to your body. As your body moves to the inside position, place your open right hand on the opponent's left. Later, counter with a right blow on the slip, then a left and right as the weave is performed.

Weaving to the outside — As the opponent leads a right punch, slip to the inside position (figure B) and place your right hand on the opponent's left. Now, move your head and body to the left and upward in a circular movement so that the opponent's right lead approximates your right shoulder. Your body is now on the outside of the opponent's lead and in the basic position (figure A). Carry both hands high and close.

Remember, weaving is based on slipping and thus, mastery of slipping helps to obtain skill in weaving. It is more difficult than slipping, but a very effective defense maneuver once perfected.

The weave is rarely used by itself. Almost invariably, the weave is used with the bob. The purpose of the *bob and weave* is to slide *under* the opponent's attack and get to close-quarters. The real bobber-weaver is always a hooking specialist. It is the perfect attack for one to use against taller opponents. Break your rhythm often when you use it. Don't be a rhythmatic bobber-weaver. Sometimes when you slip inside a punch, you counter terrifically *as you step.* Evasiveness should not be practiced without hitting or kicking to counter.

Almost every fighter at one time or another reaches a dangerous spot where he loses some of his command and must protect himself.

In addition, while the punches are coming, keep your eyes open every minute. The punches will not wait for you. They will strike unexpectedly and, unless you are trained well enough to spot them, they will be hard to stop.

The elbows and forearms are used for protection against body punches. Blows aimed at the head are swept aside by the hand when you are not sliding and countering.

Almost every fighter at one time or another reaches a dangerous spot where he loses some of his command and must protect himself. When this time comes, it is wise to have learned good defense.

ATTACK

There is nothing much in this art. Take things as they are.
Punch when you have to punch; kick when you have to kick.

ATTACK!

There is little direct attack in Jeet Kune Do. Practically all offensive action is indirect, coming after a feint or taking the form of countering after an opponent's attack is foiled or spent — it requires agile maneuvering, feinting and drawing an opponent, a scientific plan.

There are two basic moments for attack:

1. When our own will decides the time of attack.
2. When the moment of attack depends upon the opponent's movement or the failure of his action.

If a fighter *concentrates* sufficiently, *senses the moment* to attack and *acts upon it swiftly and decisively*, the prospects of success are greatly enhanced.

There will be an even better chance of success if the direct attack is launched when the opponent is moving his arm away from the line in which one wishes to attack. This is important.

Conserve your energy but attack decisively, confidently and with a single mind.

The Psychophysical Process of Attack

1. *Survey:* The survey is entirely mental and could be sub-divided into two parts.
   a. Definable: For instance, the estimation of the correct distance between the fighters or the appearance of an opening.
   b. Instinctive: Whether the opponent will attack or retire.
2. *Decision:* This is also a mental function, but the nerves and muscles are alerted in preparation for execution. During this phase, the fighter decides how to attack. For example, should it be from a short distance with a direct attack or should he, from a long distance, use a compound attack? Alternatively, he could attack with a second intention or in any other way he considers will be successful.
3. *Action:* The brain has given the muscles the order which they now execute, but even in the execution, the fighter has to be prepared for the possibility of an interception, counter, etc. Thus, it is both essential and obvious that mental and physical alertness be maintained throughout the fight.

Conserve your energy but attack decisively, confidently and with a single mind.

Primary and Secondary Attack

Primary

These are attacks initiated by oneself with the intention of scoring by *pace, fraud or force.*

Pace: A direct attack is made on the lunge to hit the opponent with superior neatness and quickness before he can parry, without any attempt to disguise the direction of the attack.

Fraud: An indirect attack may be used to deceive or evade with the first half of the thrust. A feint may precede the attack to induce your opponent, through some preliminary movement, to think that you are going to hit him in one particular line. On his offering a parry to protect that line, you may then deceive it and be free to complete the attack by lunging in another line.

Force: Upon finding your opponent covered, you attack his hand with sufficient vigor to turn it aside and make an opening for your hand on the lunge.

Secondary

These are attacks intended to out-maneuver or retaliate attacks initiated by the opponent in one or another of their different stages.

Attacks on the preparation are used to arrest his movement before he matures his plan.

Attacks on the development are principally "time" attacks. Having anticipated in what line your opponent's attack will be delivered, you intercept his arm as he begins his attack and meet him by straightening in the counter.

Attacks on the completion are made after the opponent has brought himself within thrusting range on his lunge. These *ripostes* are made from the position of the parry, whatever it may be, once the opponent's primary attack has been diverted. They may be thrown while the opponent is extended on the lunge or during his act of recovery, but they are, almost without exception, unaccompanied by any movement of the foot.

Decoy or false attacks may be used in any of the three stages as preparation for the secondary attacks. Thus used, they are *not* made with the intention of hitting the opponent, but only to lure him into, say, attacking you in some line so that you may

Attacks on the completion are made after the opponent has brought himself within thrusting range on his lunge.

disconcert him with an emphatic parry and lead up to an effective return. These attacks, therefore, are not made on the lunge for a slight movement of the foot (if any) is all that is needed.

A hit (hand or foot) is made by using the stroke which corresponds to that of the opponent, taking advantage of the opportunity to deliver it with proper timing.

Against an opponent who opens up his target or makes wild actions, for instance, counter-timing into his action or stop-kicking into his advanced target or exposed areas as he moves forward are particularly effective.

A fighter who is observant will not carry on stubbornly with strokes that are no longer the right ones. So many fighters put down the failure of an offensive stroke to a lack of speed rather than to the incorrect choice of stroke. The pro knows better.

Each fighter, therefore, has to be studied from the several angles of style, tactics and cadence before a definite plan of action involving a choice of stroke is finally decided upon.

Fighters can be placed into two main categories: the "mechanical" fighter and the "intellectual" fighter. It's easy for the mechanical fighter to give advice because his fighting techniques and tactics are the result of the mechanical repetition of strokes, bred of a lesson which was purely automatic and lacking an intelligent explanation of the *why*, the *how* and the *when*. Their fighting follows a similar pattern in each successive encounter.

The intelligent fighter will never hesitate to change tactics in order to use the correct strokes to deal with his opponent. It must be plain by now that the fighter's decision to use any particular stroke must be influenced by his opponent's technique and method of fighting.

The on-guard position, the alive, controlled parry, the timely simple attack, the sensitive, well-regulated advance and retreat, the blinding lunge and the speedy, balanced recovery must all be learned thoroughly. Acquire the appropriate neuro-muscular perception of all these so that they only require passing attention and you may be free to concentrate on your adversary, his ploy and your solution of his attack and defense. Freedom of movement, balance and confidence accompany a practiced certainty of the fundamental movements.

The intelligent fighter will never hesitate to change tactics in order to use the correct strokes to deal with his opponent.

To attack, you must study the adversary's weaknesses and strengths and take advantage of the former while avoiding the latter.

If your opponent has a good hand for parrying, for instance, the attacks should be preceded by a beat, press or feint that might disorganize the functioning of the parry.

All attacking movements must be made as small as possible; that is, with the least deviation of the hand necessary to induce the opponent to react. Caution demands that the attack should be completed covered, or augmented by any necessary defensive tactics whenever possible.

The form of an attack is generally dictated by the form of defense used by the opponent. In other words, between opponents of approximately the same caliber, an attack can rarely be successful unless it deceives or outwits the defense. For instance, an attack made with a circular movement cannot succeed if the defender meets it with a simple or lateral movement in his parry. It is, therefore, essential to correctly anticipate an opponent's reaction if the attack is to succeed. Your *final* choice of stroke should be based on your observation of the opponent's reactions, habits and preferences.

It is dangerous for a fighter to launch himself into complicated compound attacks where there are several periods of movement-time in which an opponent can land a stop-hit.

The more complicated the attack, the more chance there is of an unpremeditated counter-offensive movement being executed out of hand. This being the case, the attack proper must remain simple, whatever form the preparation may have taken.

PREPARATION OF ATTACK

Because of the wide measure the opponent maintains, the gaining of distance has to be "covered" by some action which will momentarily distract the opponent's attention. This action may be:

1. a variation of distance
2. attacks on the closer targets (usually lead leg, extended hand, groin)
3. a combination of the above two
4. a combination of attacks to disturb

To attack, you must study the adversary's weaknesses and strengths and take advantage of the former while avoiding the latter.

A preparation of attack is the action taken by the attacker to make an opening for his attack. It usually consists of some movement which will *deflect the attacking opponent's extended lead or obtain a desired reaction (for an opening) and will afford a change of distance.*

———————

An aggressive opponent can often be drawn within distance by a series of steps backward which are progressively shortened; a wary opponent can sometimes be maneuvered into the same position by a series of steps forward and backward of varying length.

———————

Fighters resort to preparations in an attempt to obtain some form of reaction from their opponents when feints have failed to fulfill that purpose.

———————

Feints preceded by beats or trappings of the hand can upset the defender's confidence and force him to move to a defensive action against his will. His defensive action may then be deceived in the attack.

———————

Beats, change-beats, engagements and changes of engagement will either fix the opponent's hand in a particular line, causing him to contract and slow down his reactions, or will make him parry sooner or with less control than he intended. Whatever the reaction, it may pave the way for a successful simple attack.

A preparation of attack is the action taken by the attacker to make an opening for his attack.

———————

By deflecting or trapping the hand while stepping forward, the possibility of a successful stop-hit from the opponent has been limited. Likewise, obstructing the leg as a preliminary step is very effective.

———————

When trapping, make sure the lines are either covered or augmented with trunk swaying or supplementary guards. The movements must be tight. Also, seize any opportunity to stop-hit or time-hit in the midst of trapping.

———————

Trapping the hand, beats or opposition on the hand can make it difficult for the adversary to parry by confusing him. Watch out for disengagement. If he is a habitual disengager, stop-hit him by first feinting the preparation, then attacking with the trap.

———————

When a step forward and an action on the opponent's hand are made simultaneously, it is known as a *compound preparation.* Its success depends on perfect coordination of both the hands and feet. Much time must be given to the practice of this type of action.

Experiment on the above with the idea of using *economical trapping* to either immobilize or draw a reaction and then, slipping in a solid, maiming thrust or kick to an extremely delicate vital spot.

_____

When advancing for the preparation of attack, pay particular attention to your balance and foot control so that you can halt your movement forward with the least possible effort. Short, rapid steps will ensure this, as your center of gravity is less likely to be shifted than if you made long and rushed steps. Do not hurl yourself at your opponent, but gain and maintain distance in a calm and precise manner.

_____

If the attack by preparation is repeated too often, it will draw a stop-hit rather than a parry. So when you do use the attack by preparation, initiate it with great economy and never open the lines more than necessary to trap. Try to shorten your period of vulnerability.

_____

By remembering that though the preparation and the attack form one smooth flow, they are actually two separate movements, the fighter will be able to take precautions against possible counterattacks.

_____

When practicing the preparations, the pupil should execute them on his partner's *engagement, change of engagement and feints.*

_____

Do not hurl yourself at your opponent, but gain and maintain distance in a calm and precise manner.

SIMPLE ATTACK

All direct and indirect attacks composed of a single movement are called "*simple attacks*" because their object is to go to the target by the most direct route.

_____

A *direct* simple attack is one made into the line of engagement or into the opposite line by simply beating the opponent to the punch, or catching him in a moment of vulnerability.

_____

An *indirect* simple attack is a single movement, the first half of which causes some reaction from the opponent so that the second half may be completed opposite the original line of engagement into the opening line.

_____

Any thrust is more likely to be successful if it is made *as the line is opening* rather than as it is being closed. An attack thrown into the opening line gains time because the opponent's action is committed to moving in the opposite direction, and he must reverse his action or alter it substantially in order to defend.

When deceiving the opponent's hand, offensive hand actions are usually made of semi-circular or circular movements.

Indirect attack often makes use of the disengagement or counter-disengagement in order to reach the opening line.

The *disengagement* is one single movement of passing the hand from the line of engagement into the opposite line, attacking from a closed line into an open one. To *time* this movement for the execution of the attack means that, for a moment, the defense is moving in an opposite direction to that of the attack. Therefore, it is while the opponent's arm is traveling across that the fighter must start his offensive action. Similar timing can be obtained from a fighter who is continually making an absence of touch and returning to engagement.

Note: Supplement the disengagement with a parry, an in-line thrust, head movement, changing of level, trunk movement, etc.

Indirect attack often makes use of the disengagement or counter-disengagement in order to reach the opening line.

When going from a high to a low line or vice versa, a supported disengagement is favored. When going from right to left or vice versa, the attacks are done by cutting over (moving diagonally *across* the opponent's line of engagement).

The following are the two types of simple attack and the movements on the opponent's part with which they must be timed. It is also a *drill* that must be returned to at regular intervals.

1. Direct attack on
   a. the absence of touch
   b. the engagement
   c. the change of engagement
   d. the step forward with and without the above

2. Indirect attack with disengagement on
   a. the beat
   b. the engagement
   c. the change of engagement
   d. the first three executed with a step forward

The counter-disengagement is the offensive movement that *corresponds* to the change of engagement or to the counter-parry. Its object is to deceive a circular movement, not a lateral movement which is the object of disengagement. Unlike the disengagement, the counter-disengagement does not end in the line opposite to that of the opponent.

———————————————————

Example: The attacker engages his opponent in sixte (attacker's high outside line). The defender disengages in a circular motion to the opposite line. The attacker follows circularly, brings the defender's hand back to the original line and attacks.

———————————————————

Remember, most people are weak in the low line. Often direct your simple attack, disengagement and counter-disengagement toward the low line. Remember also, defend while attacking!

———————————————————

If you wish to make use of *any* form of attack, the opponent's *habits* and *preferences* must be observed. Success in simple attack especially, direct or indirect, lies in correct selection. *The attack must correspond to whatever movement is being or may be made by the adversary.* Thus, it is dangerous to attack with just anything that comes to mind.

It is dangerous to attack with just anything that comes to mind.

———————————————————

The success of simple attack also depends on the correct timing of the movement, which must naturally be *related to the cadence of the opponent's movements* if it is not to be caught up in them.

———————————————————

Simple attacks started within distance of the adversary should land, if properly made, provided the adversary does not supplement the parry by retreating. Thus, to be safe, induce the opponent to step forward into the "within distance area" and nail him while he is stepping or merely shifting his weight forward, or when he shows any sign of "weightiness," mentally or physically.

———————————————————

Use an "innocently detached rhythm" with the opponent. Once into the attack, concentrate on the determination to land with mechanical efficiency and correct timing.

———————————————————

To ensure the success of a simple attack, coordinate all into a powerful *one*. Maintain a continuous looseness throughout and develop *smooth* explosive speed. Relax! Any tension while awaiting the opportunity to launch the attack (through correctly found distance) will only give a short, jerky movement, will cause you to move too soon or will give the opponent an indication of your intention. This fact cannot be stressed too often. *Relaxation* will bring about *smoothness, precision* and *speed*. Don't forget.

Before initiation — Stay loose but poised.

Initiation — Be economical; use one continuous movement from a state of neutrality.

In flight — Employ the most economical use of movement and force along the most direct line of attack, backed by tight covering.

After initiation — Use a quick, natural flow to recover the small phasic bent-knee position.

Emphasize a repetitious drilling of economical form to acquire instinctive initiation, speed and length of power and penetration. Remember that acceleration can be increased by sheer practice and will power. Mechanical repetition is the basis of this. Lunge two or three hundred times per day, faster and faster each time.

It is important to recognize that no amount of science can compensate for the lack of striking power, and powerful hitting is terribly discounted unless it is well-timed, rapid and accurate.

Thus, the first step for anyone is learning to hit and kick properly with either limb. Hitting and kicking must also be taught in conjunction with footwork.

Nothing bothers an adversary more than *variety* in both attack and defense.

Nothing bothers an adversary more than *variety* in both attack and defense, and it eases physical strain by constantly shifting the onus of exertion from one group of muscles to another.

Likewise, nothing is more dangerous than a half-hearted attack; let your attacks fly, concerning yourself only with the correct and most determined execution of your offensive.

While attacking, you should look as boldly aggressive as a beast of prey — without becoming reckless — in order to bring pressure at once upon the adversary's morale. Possess the eye of an eagle, the cunning of a fox, the agility and alertness of a cat with the courage, aggressiveness and fierceness of a panther, the striking power of a cobra and the resistance of a mongoose.

Simple attack will not always be successful against every opponent. Other means will have to be devised as well. Learn as many varied defensive moves and as many useful and varied hits as possible; then, you will be able to cope with varied styles as they come along.

COMPOUND ATTACK

Between fighters of equal speed and technique whose judgments of distance are maintained correctly, a simple attack is extremely difficult to bring off. The fighter has to solve the problem of making up his disadvantage in distance and, simultaneously, gaining time. By the use of compound attack, he can do so.

Compound attacks consist of more than one action and may be initiated first by a feint, a preparation on the hand or an attack on a closer target, followed immediately by the real attack.

The first movement in a combination should start from the small phasic bent-knee stance. It should be initiated from an economical flow without telegraphing — a smooth, surprising extension.

Basically, compound attacks are a combination of the four forms of simple attack: thrusts, simple disengagements, counter-disengagements and cut-overs.

Compound attacks may be of no avail if they are badly timed or if a favorable opportunity is not seized.

The complexity of the compound attack used is directly related to the opponent's ability to parry the offensive movements made. When choosing the strokes to be used in a compound attack, success will depend on a correct anticipation of the form of parry (front hand or rear hand, lateral or circular) which the opponent will make in answer to the feint or first attack. Before using a compound attack, therefore, it is essential to *observe* and gain some idea of the opponent's likely reaction.

Feints must be made sufficiently to impress the opponent. Also, employ the least number of feints necessary to achieve success. The more complicated the form of the compound attack, the less chance it has of being successful. It is dangerous to attempt attacks composed of more than two feints.

Simple compound attacks, those comprised of just one feint or prior offensive action (one-two, low-high, etc.) will have all the more chance of success if they are delivered on the opponent's preparation, in particular on the step forward.

Compound attacks may be of no avail if they are badly timed or if a favorable opportunity is not seized.

Many compound attacks fail because the attacker forgets to *regulate the speed of his feints* in such a way that they are moving *just ahead of the offensive movement.* Thus, it is essential to find both cadence and preferences in the opponent's defense.

Compound attacks may be:

1. short, fast combinations. *Crispy*
2. deep, penetrative (and fast) combinations. *Uncrispy*

All blows strive to exert maximum force *for what they are worth;* that is why some need more forceful reinforcement. Thus, the idea of combinations.

Be exposed to the various paths of combinations and be able to change paths during execution.

During gaps of combinations, insert:

1. *non-commitments* to distract the opponent, or to improve positioning or the flow.
2. *delicacy* to score without destroying the overall balance and flow of the combination (finger jabs, finger fan, finger flicks, backhand, palm thrust).

It is essential to find both cadence and preferences in the opponent's defense.

Use double leads against a man who is slow on his feet or who is exhausted.

Some boxing combinations (preceded by feints):

1. right jab/left cross (one-two)
2. right jab/right uppercut
3. right jab/left cross/right hook
4. right jab/right uppercut/right hook
5. right jab/right hook
6. right jab/body hook
7. left body thrust/right hook
8. left body thrust/right body hook

Combinations with Kicking

Find kicks most economical for yourself and those most direct to the opponent. Use the on-guard position for guidance. Kicks in compound attacks may have several purposes.

To disorganize

1. Hook kick to knee, low stomping side kick, lead hand finger jab, rear hand cross or preparation on opponent's hand (trapping)
2. Direct, fast, groin hook kick to . . .
   # Don't take eyes off opponent.
   # Don't commit to point of difficulty in recovery.
   # Remember on-guard positioning!
3. Shin/knee counter stop-kick to . . .
   # at opponent's initiation
   # during development
   # at completion (in riposte)
4. Low hand strike to high lead hook kick (against right stancer)
5. Low hand strike to high reverse hook kick (with rear leg)
6. Feint high, hook kick low
7. Feint hook kick low, strike high
8. Feint side, spinning back kick
9. Feint side kick, hook kick (lead foot)
10. Feint lead straight kick, hook kick (lead foot)
11. Rear foot sweep feint, lead hook kick

To harass

1. Direct, fast, groin hook kick and . . .
2. Direct, fast, shin/knee side kick and . . .

The follow-up would be affected by whether the opponent is caught flatfooted or on the way back.

To force

1. Double stepping shin/knee side kick
2. Side kick led by a reverse hook with the hand
3. Hook kick led by a reverse hook with the hand
4. Pursuing side kicks and hook kicks

Find kicks most economical for yourself and those most direct to the opponent.

When studying combinations of kicks and hands, re-examine the idea of the most economical moves for yourself and those moves most direct to the opponent in light of combination movement.

Shift back and forth from leg to hand, from hand to leg and vary the heights. Go high/low, low/high or safety triples (low/high/low, high/low/high).

Use *natural* follow-ups between the lead hand (jab, hook, backfist, shovel path) and the rear hand (straight, cross, overhand, hammer). Likewise, find the *natural* follow-ups between the lead leg (side kick, hook, straight, upward, reverse, vertical, horizontal) and the rear leg (straight thrusts at various heights, spin kicks, hooks at various heights). What are the natural follow-ups between hand and leg or leg and hand?

Examine the possibilities in all branches of footwork — advancing, retreating, circling right, circling left, additional movements like parallel sliding.

Examine the natural follow-ups for blows that miss or fall short and study their defensive accompaniments. Explore the types of opponent reactions to a miss.

Nurse the on-guard position. Examine all the physical movements in order to facilitate returning quickly to the on-guard position and being able to attack and defend from wherever you end up or could end up.

> Counterattacking is a subtle art, *safer* to the man using it and more *damaging* to his opponent.

COUNTERATTACK

(A)

(B)

The use of the left hand in *countering* the right

Counterattacking is a subtle art, *safer* to the man using it and more *damaging* to his opponent. Attacking by force sometimes does little damage because the opponent is

173

moving in the same direction as the force. His going with the punches removes their sting.

With two evenly-matched competitors, the advantage lies with the man who counters because when a man leads, he cannot help but expose more than the one who remains on-guard. Any commitment automatically opens an *invitation* or target area.

Any commitment automatically opens an *invitation* or target area.

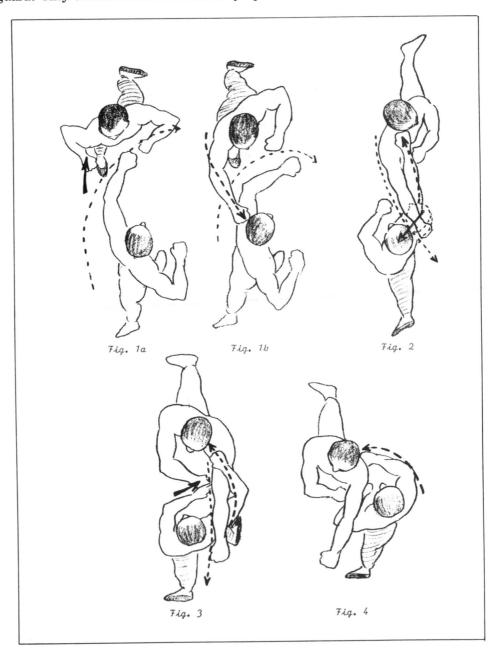

Fig. 1a   Fig. 1b   Fig. 2

Fig. 3   Fig. 4

Instead of making a false attack, change of engagement, trapping or beating the hand, the *invitation* may be used to *provoke* the opponent to attack. The provoker may then parry, block or avoid the opponent's attack and follow with a counterattack. A double hit is the result of the opponent using the same tactic, making an invitation with the first hit and hitting into his adversary as he tries to counter. An invitation may also be performed by purposely leaving a target area open while in the defensive position.

To counter, you must avoid being hit and succeed in hitting your opponent while he is still *out of position* as the result of missing you. You must act *instinctively* and *instantaneously*. This is possible through faithful drilling. Once you learn to counter instinctively, you can devote your awareness to your broad plan of battle.

According to boxing, avoiding your opponent's lead, the first part of counterfighting, may be done in three ways:

1. Make him miss by slipping it, ducking it or drawing away from it.
2. You can guard or deflect straight punches by turning them away from you, causing them to miss and expend themselves.
3. You can block the punch with a part of your body which can stand this punching — few blocks are recommended. It is much better for you and more tiring for the opponent if he misses.

Once you learn to counter instinctively, you can devote your awareness to your broad plan of battle.

Any active man can be taught to lead and recover with power and rapidity because the motions are more or less mechanical and he can choose his own time for starting the "machinery." It is far different with countering; the "leader" chooses the time and also that portion of his target about to be exposed. The man who counters is in a somewhat similar position to one who starts a race at his opponent's "Go!"

Anticipation is the secret of countering and therefore it is preferable to feint your man into making a lead rather than to wait for him to do so.

A counterattack is an offensive action delivered on the opponent's attack in such a way that it gains a period of "movement-time" from it.

Counters are simple combinations of the most elementary defensive and offensive moves.

- # Avoidance of the opponent's lead by defensive means.
- # Delivery of corresponding counter hits.

The counter-attack calls for the greatest skill, the most perfect planning and the most delicate execution of all fighting techniques.

Samples

LEAD	COUNTER
1. jab	1. snap back, counter jab
2. jab	2. slip outside, counter jab
3. lead swing or hook	3. guard with rear forearm and counter jab
4. jab	4. push aside with rear hand shovel body hook with lead
5. rear swing or hook	5. beat opponent to punch with fast jab
6. jab	6. slip inside, rear hand body blow for counter
7. jab	7. slip inside, left cross
8. lead swing or hook	8. beat opponent to punch with left cross
9. rear cross	9. duck under, counter to groin or weave to left body thrust
10. rear cross or swing	10. guard with lead forearm, return with left jab

---

When practicing counters, first, work on good form and later, on speed.

Always follow up and press your advantage after countering until the opponent goes down or fights back.

The counterattack is not a defensive action but a method of using an opponent's offense as a means to the successful completion of one's own attack. The counter-attack is an advanced phase of offense requiring a foreknowledge of specific openings which will result from attack by the opponent.

The counterattack calls for the greatest skill, the most perfect planning and the most delicate execution of all fighting techniques. It uses as tools all the main techniques: blocking, guarding, parrying, slipping, bobbing and weaving, ducking, sidestepping, feinting, drawing and shifting. It uses all phases of grappling, kicking and hitting. Besides a mastery of techniques, the counterattack requires exact timing, unerring judgment and cool, calculating poise. It means careful thought, daring execution and sure control. It is the greatest art in fighting, the art of the champion.

There are numerous counters which may be used for every lead, but for each particular occasion, there is one counter that is most effective in that situation. Action must be instantaneous and where there is a wide choice of action, instant action is difficult, if not impossible, unless the right action has been previously conditioned. Conditioning (guided by overall awareness), then, becomes the keystone of the counterattack.

Conditioning is a process whereby a specific stimulus will cause a specific reaction. A repeated stimulus eventually creates an action pattern in the nervous system. Once this pattern is established, the mere presence of the stimulus will cause the specific action. Such action is instantaneous and almost unconscious, which is necessary for effective countering. Conditioned action should be the result of intense and concentrated practice of planned action patterns in response to every lead.

Such action should be practiced slowly for hours, days, weeks, always in response to certain leads. Finally, the lead itself will automatically bring the right counter.

Fighting should be done with the head, not with the hands or feet. It is true that during the time of actual fighting, one does not think of how to fight but rather, of the weakness or strength of the opponent, of possible openings and opportunities. Fighting will never reach the stage of a true art unless performance of skill is made automatic and the cortex freed to think and to associate, to make plans and to judge. The higher nerve centers always retain control and will act when necessary. It is like pressing a button to start or stop a machine.

Conditioning is a process whereby a specific stimulus will cause a specific reaction.

In a consideration of countering, there are three factors that must be understood:

1. the lead of the opponent
2. the method of avoiding the lead
3. the counterblow, kick or grappling itself

---

1. *The lead of the opponent* is important in that it *determines the side of the body open to attack.* A right lead exposes the right side of the body, while a lead with the rear hand exposes almost all of the upper trunk.

2. *To avoid leads*, it must be decided whether the counterattack should be one or two-handed. Blocking, guarding, stopping, parrying, all leave one hand with which to counter. Such maneuvers as slipping, sidestepping, ducking, bobbing and weaving, feinting, drawing, and shifting allow a two-handed attack.

3. The counter blow depends on the method used in avoiding the opponent's lead as well as upon the lead itself.

    First: have opponent committed and out of form.

Second:　fit in harmoniously to form a single functional unit.

Third:　coordinate all power to attack his weakness.

Right Lead Hand Counters for a Straight Right Lead

By blocking or stopping

1.　Catch the opponent's lead in your left hand while stepping right, then drive a straight right lead to his chin.

By parrying

1.　Parry to the outside guard position and hook the right to his solar plexus.
2.　Parry to the outside position and hook the right to his chin.
3.　Parry to the outside position and deliver a right shovel hook to his chin.
4.　Parry to the inside position and drive a straight right lead to his chin.
5.　Parry to the inside position and hook the right to his solar plexus.
6.　Parry to the inside position and deliver a right shovel hook to his solar plexus.

Fit in harmoniously to form a single functional unit.

By slipping

1.　Slip to the outside guard position and hook the right to his chin.
2.　Slip to the outside position and hook the right to his solar plexus.
3.　Slip to the outside position and drive a right uppercut to his solar plexus.
4.　Slip to the outside position and drive a straight right to his chin.

By sidestepping

1.　Sidestep to the outside guard position and hook the right to his chin.
2.　Sidestep to the outside position and hook the right to his solar plexus.
3.　Sidestep to the outside position and drive a right uppercut to his chin.
4.　Sidestep to the outside position and drive a straight right lead to his chin.

Left Rear Hand Counters for a Straight Right Lead

By parrying

1.　Parry to the inside guard position with the left hand, then drive the left hand to the opponent's chin.
2.　Cross-parry with the right hand to the inside position and drive a straight left to his side.

By slipping

1. Slip to the inside guard position and hook the left to his body.
2. Slip to the inside position and drive a straight left to his body.
3. Slip to the inside position and drive a straight left to his chin.
4. Slip to the inside position and cross a left hook to his chin.
5. Slip to the inside position and drive a straight left to his solar plexus.

By sidestepping

1. Sidestep to the outside guard position and drive a left cross to his chin.
2. Sidestep to the outside position and drive a left to his body.
3. Sidestep to the inside position and drive a left uppercut to his chin.
4. Sidestep to the inside position and drive a left shovel hook to his chin.
5. Sidestep to the inside position and drive a left uppercut to his solar plexus.

Right Lead Hand Counters for a Straight Left Rear Lead

By parrying

1. Cross parry with the left hand to the inside guard position and hook the right to his chin.
2. Cross parry with the left hand to the inside position and hook the right to his abdomen.

Coordinate all power to attack his weakness.

By slipping

1. Slip to the inside guard position and hook the right to his solar plexus.
2. Slip to the inside position and hook the right to his chin.
3. Slip to the outside position and cross the right to his chin or body.

By sidestepping

1. Sidestep to the inside guard position and drive a straight right to his chin.

Left Rear Hand Counters for a Straight Left Rear Lead

By parrying

1. Parry with the right hand to the inside guard position and drive a straight left to his chin or body.

2.   Parry with the right hand to the inside position and hook the left to his chin or body.
3.   Parry with the right hand to the inside position and drive a left uppercut to his chin or solar plexus.
4.   Parry with the right hand to the outside position and hook the left to his chin or solar plexus.
5.   Parry with the right hand to the outside position and drive a left uppercut to his chin or solar plexus.

By slipping

1.   Slip to the outside guard position and hook the left to his chin or body.
2.   Slip to the outside position and drive a left uppercut to his chin or body.
3.   Slip to the outside position and drive a straight left to his face or body.
4.   Slip to the inside position and drive a left shovel hook to his solar plexus.

By sidestepping

1.   Sidestep to the outside guard position and hook the left to his chin or body.
2.   Sidestep to the outside and drive a left uppercut to his solar plexus.

The inside parry
and right hook
to the body is a
jarring, sickening
blow used to slow
up an opponent.

The inside parry and right jab is a straight right timed so as to take advantage of the opening left by the opponent's jab. It is a fundamental counter used consciously or unconsciously by almost every fighter. It is used to avoid the opponent's jab and, at the same time, to sting and jar him. It is used to set up openings for other counters as well. *It is used best against a slow jab.*

The outside parry and right jab is a jab delivered after slipping the opponent's lead over the right shoulder. It is a safe way to avoid a right lead while dealing out punishment at the same time. It is best used against the long-armed opponent as it adds length to the right arm. The right jab is parried and held momentarily to the right shoulder. The more the opponent steps in with his jab, the more severely he will be hit. *It should be used in combination with jabbing from the inside position.*

The inside parry and right hook to the body is a jarring, sickening blow used to slow up an opponent. It is rather dangerous to execute as it brings the body within range of the opponent's left hand. As the right hand and shoulder drop, the right side of your body becomes a target for the opponent. Therefore, it must be used suddenly and depends entirely upon speed and deception for its success.

The outside parry and right hook is used to bring down the opponent's guard to create openings for the left hand and to slow up an opponent. It is easy, safe and effective. It often becomes an uppercut rather than a hook.

The inside block and left hook *is first a block* and then, a blow. It should be used against a slow jab or *against the fighter who carries his right lead hand well out from his shoulder.* It is a powerful blow but requires more practice and more accurate timing than most counters. It requires blocking a right lead from the inside, then shifting the weight forward and hooking the left to the chin. It is not advisable to use unless the opening is apparent.

The left cross is one of the most talked about blows in Western boxing and is the counter most often used by all boxers. Delivered properly, it exerts terrific force. It is merely a left hook to the jaw crossed over an opponent's extended straight right lead. The opponent's jab is slipped over the left shoulder and the left hand is then hooked from the outside across to the chin. It is easy to execute and is really a finishing blow.

The straight inside left is a straight left timed to cross *under* and *inside* an opponent's right lead. It is best used against an opponent who steps well in with his right lead and particularly in conjunction with the outside parry and right jab or right cross. It is a set-up or finishing blow, is easy to time and carries terrific power. The right hand must be carried high, in position to stop or guard.

A riposte is an attack (or more accurately a counterattack) following a parry.

The inside left to the ribs is a sucker punch in that it takes advantage of a natural opening created by any right lead. It is difficult to guard against. It is a straight left timed so as to drive underneath an opponent's right arm as he jabs and is used to slow up an opponent or to "shorten his arm."

To minimize danger of a counter:

1.   Feint to disturb your opponent's rhythm, causing him to "un-set" as well as lose a period of movement-time.
2.   Change your body position during attack by slipping left and right, changing levels suddenly (ducking), swaying (bob and weave).
3.   Use a constantly changing variety of attacks and defenses.

RIPOSTE

A riposte is an attack (or more accurately a counterattack) following a parry.

The choice of riposte, like the choice of attack, is determined by the type of defensive movement one thinks that the opponent is likely to adopt against it. *The opponent's reactions can only be ascertained by observing his usual hand movements when recovering from an unsuccessful attack.*

Direct riposte is delivered in the same line as that of the parry. It is comprised of only one direct movement (in-line covering, supplementary defense, trunk movement, etc.). The choice of using direct riposte rests on the reaction and habits of the opponent — observe, deduce and apply the correct stroke.

Indirect riposte (by disengagement, counter-disengagement, cut-over) is made in the line opposite to that of the parry by passing the hand under, over or around the opponent's hand. It is used against a fighter who covers after being parried. Make it smooth, economical and covered.

Types of Riposte

The immediate *riposte* is the most effective as it forces the opponent to be on the defensive.

1. SIMPLE RIPOSTE
   a. direct
   b. indirect

2. COMPOUND RIPOSTE
   a. composed of one or more feints

3. Simple or compound ripostes terminating in the low line

Any of these ripostes can be executed *immediately* after a parry, or can be *delayed*. Also, the riposte can be given with or without the help of a lunge. Whether the lunge should be used is determined solely by the opponent's speed of recovery from the attack.

Generally, the *immediate riposte* is the most effective as it forces the opponent to be on the defensive. To ensure its effectiveness, the parry and riposte must be made just as the attack is ending and before the opponent has an opportunity to change from offense to defense. This form is known as "parrying and riposting on the final of the attack," and implies that the defender is morally certain of the line in which the attack will end. The immediate riposte on the final of the attack may be done crispy, into a direct combination, or it may be non-crispy to adhere and maim.

The *delayed riposte* is where one hesitates in his choice of riposte after the parry, looking for his opponent's reaction. The opponent, used to a direct riposte, might automatically go for a parry and, in finding no hand, is apt to become flustered by this change of cadence and lose some control in his defense. The delayed riposte may be a combination attack or one with feinting.

Applications of simple riposte:

1. The *direct riposte* is executed against a fighter who, when on the lunge, commits the error of bending his arm preparatory to recovery, thus leaving himself exposed in the line of the parry.

2. The *indirect riposte* (by disengagement or cut-over) is used against an opponent who, expecting a direct riposte, covers in the line in which he has been parried. Sometimes he covers intentionally; often it is merely an instinctive movement. Whatever the reason, if this covering is successful, the riposter must anticipate and deceive it by a simple disengagement.

3. The *riposte by counter-disengagement* is made against an opponent who, when on the lunge or recovering, does not remain in the line of the parry, but changes his engagement — in other words, takes a counter. The counter-disengagement deceives his change of engagement. This form of riposte is particularly useful from the right stance when dealing with a left stancer.

4. The *riposte in low line* is the choice made against an opponent who ends his attacks correctly covered and who recovers with his arm extended, thus, leaving only his lower target open.

Knowing the nature of an opponent's stroke, it will not be difficult to time it and turn it to one's advantage.

The *compound riposte* is a counter offensive movement after the parry composed of one or more feints. Example:

> Compound riposte of one-two, following the parry of counter sixte — The attacker, having been brought back to the line of sixte by the counter and anticipating the direct riposte, covers in sixte. The riposter, then, maintaining his bent arm, feints a disengagement, draws the attacker's parry of quarte and, still with a bent arm, deceives it, finally thrusting the riposte in sixte.

Again, *timing is all-important.* A parry and riposte are most effective if made *as the attack is completing its course.* At this point, the time available to the opponent to change from attack to defense is cut to the minimum. Consequently, the riposte has the best chance to succeed before the attacker can parry it.

By reacting purposely to an opponent's *exploratory moves* in one definite way, it is often possible to induce him to use a particular stroke. Knowing the nature of his stroke, it will not be difficult to time it and turn it to one's advantage.

The *counter-riposte* is an offensive movement which follows a successful parry of the riposte. It can be delivered by either the attacker or the defender and can be simple or compound. It can be executed while on the lunge, while recovering, after having recovered or without a lunge, according to the distance.

--- · ---

Counter-riposte may be the result of *second intention*. By second intention, we mean that the original attack has been made, not with the object of hitting, but only to draw a parry and riposte from the defender in order to riposte from it in turn. This succession of offensive and defensive actions executed by the attacker is usually used against an opponent whose original defense is very strong, and where it is hoped that a second offensive action will catch him unprepared. The attacker can make either a half recovery after the initial false attack or shift the weight of his body back to his rear leg when parrying. Thus, he places himself out of range of the dangerous riposte. He can then counter-riposte with a half-lunge or by leaning his body forward.

Many fighters commit the error of leaning back on their rear leg when defending themselves.

RENEWED ATTACK

When the opponent retreats without troubling to parry, the redoublement (in boxing) or remise (in fencing) can be useful. It is a renewed attack or replacement of the weapon on the target in the same line as that of the original offensive or counter-offensive action. It is a stroke that may also be aimed at an advanced target such as the shin or knee and is designed to penalize an opponent who, riposting indirectly or compoundly, uncovers himself because his movements are too wide.

--- · ---

The renewed attack is very effective against fighters who, although having a strong defense, hesitate to riposte or are slow in doing so. Often, this is because they tried to parry but were off-balance.

--- · ---

And, many fighters commit the error of leaning back on their rear leg when defending themselves instead of taking a short step back. In such cases, attack the rear weight-bearing foot.

The success of a renewed attack depends, to a very great extent, on the rapidity of the recovery forward (footwork again!). The opponent must not be allowed to regain any loss of balance (physical or psychological) or control which the initial attack may have cost him.

Generally, the recovery forward is accompanied by an attack on the arms. The advantages are:

1. filling in the time lag caused by the recovery forward.
2. occupying the opponent's mind during that period and thus, minimizing the risk that he might stop-hit or riposte belatedly.
3. finding some degree of support by holding the opponent's arm during recovery.

Although a renewed attack on the spur of the moment is possible, to do so does not make certain that a period of *movement-time* will be gained. In most cases, its use as a stroke is premeditated as a result of observing the opponent's habits and tactics.

Following the recovery forward, the renewed attack itself may include the following examples:

Tactics are the brainwork of fighting.

1. straight thrust
2. feint of a straight thrust followed by an indirect simple attack or a compound attack
3. a preparation on the hand (beat, trap) followed by a simple or compound attack

---

TACTICS

Tactics are the brainwork of fighting. They are based on observation and analysis of the opponent and on intelligent choices of actions against him. The tactical approach

consists of three parts: *preliminary analysis, preparation and execution.*

Preliminary analysis: The purpose of the preliminary analysis is to lay the foundation by scrutinizing the opponent's habits, virtues and faults. The fighter should know whether his opponent is aggressive or defensive, whether he likes to make action *on time* and what his favorite attacks and parries are. Observe him closely, for even if you know him, a fighter's physical and mental condition varies from day to day. The tactical fighter should shorten and lengthen the distance and make use of false attacks that are persuasive enough to force the opponent to reveal the quality and speed of his reactions.

The tactical approach consists of three parts: preliminary analysis, preparation and execution.

Body Blows

The two basic body blows

The Combination of Low & High Right --
setting the timing with the opponent

The body feint as a mean to increase the power of right to chin

The Shift--a technique to confuse
the opponent as well as adding
power to the punch

Preparation: It is during the preparation of the action that each fighter looks for cues and tries to outwit his opponent. The variations are endless, but a few examples may be pointed out. For instance, the fighter who plans to score on the attack has to take the initiative and keep control of the play. He attempts to mislead his opponent by sometimes making a false attack followed by a real attack to a different area or to the same target area. The lines and positions should be varied in order not to give the opponent a free moment in which to seize the initiative.

The preparation of the attack should be cautious and the fighter must always be ready to parry if the opponent tries to make a sudden stop-hit or counterattack.

Execution: The execution of the real attack must be done with proper timing, quickly, without break or hesitation. It must be a conscious, accelerated, determined and decisive movement. Surprise is vital and the fighter must believe in its successful outcome. If the opponent takes the initiative, the fighter must discourage him by constant threat of counterattack, by short thrusts or strikes, by beating his guard or by other means which will disturb his concentration.

If physical qualities between fighters are equal, intellectual superiority helps to achieve victory. Between equally intelligent fighters, mechanical and technical knowledge can be decisive.

A fighter must reach a fair standard of technical ability before he can apply tactics successfully.

A fighter must reach a fair standard of technical ability before he can apply tactics successfully. Once the mechanics can be made automatically, only then can the mind concentrate on discovering the opponent's reactions, anticipating his intentions and devising the strategy and tactics required to beat him.

Tactics require cool judgment, anticipation, opportunism, bluff and counter-bluff and *the ability to think at least one move ahead.* These are combined with courage and the controlled reaction of muscles and limbs which enable the fighter to carry out simple or complex movements as required by the situation at any given moment.

It has been said that the fighter's thoughts and actions must be like one flash of lightning. Coordination of mind and body is certainly the secret of success in fighting. Mechanical perfection is useless in fighting without the ability to think and, likewise, the most intelligent analysis of an opponent's game will not ensure success unless the requisite fighting stroke can be devised and applied in the proper manner.

The basic key to fighting tactics is to take advantage of the weakness of the opponent.

Would you attack an opponent when he is all prepared, well-balanced and is either in a nervous, wild rhythm or in a well-controlled, educated rhythm? Would you meet an angered, rushing opponent head-on? Of course not! A great artist would first control distance through adjusting footwork and then, proceed to lead the opponent's rhythm through feints, false attacks and economical peckings.

It is important to always oppose the opposite tactics to those favored by the opponent (box a fighter, fight a boxer). It is obviously unwise to continually attack a fighter who relies on his defense, while one should attack without respite the opponent who favors using strong and speedy attacks. Counter-time is the answer to the stop-hit addict and the stop-hit is a counter to the fighter who uses many feints.

A fighter with a long reach or one who continually makes renewed attacks, or attacks with a step forward, generally requires a wide measure. It is a mistake to always step back on the attack or preparations, since this will help the opponent to obtain the space he requires to maneuver. Such an opponent will probably be disconcerted and lose his precision if the measure is shortened by a step forward into his attack.

A shorter man tries to make up for his shorter reach by using attacks on the hand as preparation, or attacks on advanced (closer) targets, or goes into in-fighting, if he is stronger.

Play with your own cadence to confuse the opponent, then suddenly put on a burst of speed. The fundamental tactic is to draw the opponent to step forward and attack as he steps.

A fighter cannot use the same actions against every opponent. A good man should vary his game with simple and complex attacks and counterattacks with changes of distance, etc.

Against a calm, quiet fighter, the feints must be longer; against a nervous fighter, the feints must be shorter. With the calm fighter, one should remain calm; the nervous type should be agitated (while the fighter himself tries to remain calm). Tall fighters

The basic key to fighting tactics is to take advantage of the weakness of the opponent.

are usually slower, but their long reaches are dangerous, so it is essential to keep a safe distance (until the inside position can be taken).

―――――――――――――――

Unconventional fighters use wide, sometimes unexpected motions. Against such fighters one must keep his distance and the parries should be taken at the very last moment. Unorthodox fighters usually use simple actions and almost always execute these in the same tempo. The attacks are made with wide movements, giving a chance for timed or stop-hits. The loss of a fight against such an opponent frequently points to the fighter's inflexibility and his inability to adapt his style to the requirements of the moment.

―――――――――――――――

Against an opponent who habitually attacks with a preparation on the hand which he times to perfection, fighting with an absence of touch and varying the measure, in preference to giving the hand or using an extended on-guard position, will often disconcert the opponent and severely limit his game.

―――――――――――――――

Against a patient fighter who remains well-covered on-guard, who keeps out of distance and evades any attempt to make preparation, it is unsafe to attack directly. Such fighters generally make accurate stop-kicks or hits. The obvious answer is to *draw* his stop-hit with menacing feints and complete a second-intention attack, taking his hand, maybe to grappling.

A good man should vary his game with simple and complex attacks and counter-attacks with changes of distance, etc.

―――――――――――――――

Before attacking an opponent who fences with an absence of touch, false attacks or well-marked feints can be used to draw his reaction. If this is a stop-hit, one can proceed in counter-time, preferably taking the hand. If he reacts with a parry, one can complete a compound attack or score by counter-riposte. On the other hand, the effect may be for him to return to engagement, when an appropriate attack can be made.

―――――――――――――――

The novice's rhythm, probably irregular, is hard to gauge, rendering long phrases dangerous, as he is unlikely to follow the lead being given him. He will most certainly panic easily and parry at the slightest provocation. These parries, started too soon and lacking control, often take the form of whips directed in no particular direction. They are apt to catch the attacker's arm. There is, therefore, every reason to be careful *not to attack with compound movements against a novice, but to wait for the opportunity to launch simple, rapid, economical technique.*

―――――――――――――――

Quite unintentionally, the novice will deliver *broken-rhythm* attacks, which will fool the more experienced fighter who will not be expecting such a rhythm. Thus, it is es-

sential to maintain a very carefully judged measure, which will force the novice, finally, to over-reach to hit.

A golden rule is never to use more complex movements than are necessary to achieve the desired result. Start with simple movements and only introduce compound ones when you cannot otherwise succeed. To hit a worthy opponent with a complex movement is satisfying and shows one's mastery of technique; to hit the same opponent by a simple movement is a sign of greatness.

Half the battle is won when one knows what the adversary is doing. If, in spite of having correctly chosen the corresponding movements, the action fails, the reason must be due to faulty techniques.

Repeat! A good fighter knows every stroke.

Knowing that opponents are constantly trying to note one's habits and weaknesses, it is obvious that a conscious effort must be made to give variety to one's game (including the use of feigning certain habits and weaknesses).

Right-hander versus left-hander:

The right hook is very effective as an offensive punch, and as a counter punch thrown immediately after a short hop back. Remember, a southpaw who uses his right hand efficiently along with his normally effective left hand is hard to beat.

The right-hander must keep his right hand slightly higher and either beat the left-hander to the punch with a sharp left, or feint with a left-hand punch, hop back, and then counter with a sharp left, followed by a right hook.

Another version is to keep moving to the right, using the right hand a lot for defense and the left for attacks to the head and body, more especially to the latter.

Slipping outside a left-stancer's elongated left arm or outside his left lead and countering with a long left hook to the body is good stuff.

Gliding in to trap in the engagement of the outside line is advisable before a low side kick attack on an extended target. Lean well away from his lead hand while you side

A golden rule is never to use more complex movements than are necessary to achieve the desired result.

190

kick. Economy-flow starting should eliminate his counter lead kick, especially if the flow is timed with him shifting his weight forward. Watch that his shifting is not a preparation to shooting a rear front snap kick. In this case, you should circle to your right as you glide. You might then follow with another lead backfist or whatever in another movement period.

A beat in the engagement of the outside line can be used as preparation for a false shin/knee kick, immediately using the one-and-a-half rhythm to finish the lead thrust to the opponent's face, over his hand. Use a corresponding supplementary guard for either his disengagement to a left lead hook or to a right cross.

During glides and beats in the engagement of the inside lines of the left-hander before any attack, watch out for his right leg and cross. You can minimize his rear thrusts by using an economical initiation in the first three inches of your movement. Then, circle to your right while using the preparation of your attack.

Parry and counter parry him to your high inside line.

Study slipping the left-hander's left jab while thrusting your right fist to his exposed armpit.

Half the battle is won when one knows what the adversary is doing.

Engage him on the high inside line to disengage and return on his high or low outside line. This will compel him to use his weak parries — his high outside parry or slower circular, high inside parry. If the attack is to his outside low line, he will use a low parry, leaving himself open in the high line. This can become very effective if your attack to the low line was a feint.

Fighting is a game of timing, tactics and bluff. Two of the most effective means to this are:

1. *The simple attack from immobility.* This will often surprise the opponent, especially after a series of false attacks and feints have been executed. The defender is subconsciously expecting a preparation or more complex movement and fails to react in time to the swift and unannounced simple movement.

2. *The variation of rhythm or cadence made prior to or during an attack.* This may achieve the same element of surprise. For example, a series of judiciously sloweddown feints and slow gaining and breaking ground may be used to "put the opponent to sleep." A final movement that suddenly erupts at highest speed will often take him unawares. Again, some rapid feints followed by a deliberately slowed-down or brokentime final movement will often disconcert a vigilant opponent.

Some fighters form the habit of withdrawing the hand or foot when a hit is directed towards it. Such fighters are vulnerable to an immediate renewal of the attack by a quick lunge.

To box successfully, you must see everything that goes on in the course of your fight.

Sometimes, a number of feints in the high line can pave the way for a sudden disengagement to the knee.

Preparation on the knee and trapping the hand or foot while obstructing the opponent's leg are much used to reduce the movement-time factor. Conversely, attacks on preparation are particularly effective.

A broken-time attack, making a pause before delivering the final movement, can be very effective in deceiving the opponent as to the attacker's intention.

One way to find the opponent's reaction is to launch a simple attack just out of distance so he will still have to parry. Wait for his riposte, deflect it and carefully select the target area for the counter-parry

---

Watch your opponent! Never look away from him during the actual fighting. To box successfully, you must see everything that goes on in the course of your fight. The place to watch in long-range fighting is your opponent's eyes. Notice where animals look when they fight. When in-fighting, look either at your opponent's feet or at his waist.

Take the play away from your opponent and try to get him on the defensive; keep him guessing what you are going to do next. Don't give him any rest if you can help it. Hit from all angles. When jabbing with your right, make it a double shot. Discover your opponent's weakness. Find out what bothers him the most. Concentrate your attack on that flaw in his defense and never ease up. Make him fight the type of contest he fights worst.

Keep moving, thereby preventing him from getting set to punch and making him miss. Circle and sidestep his rushes. When he gets off balance, be all over him. Follow up advantages.

Don't waste motion. Have a purpose in every action of deception, defense or attack. Don't telegraph any punches.

\# Attack with confidence.

\# Attack with accuracy.

\# Attack with great speed.

In retrospect, all aggressive arm actions, no matter how simple or complex, stem from one or more of three fundamentals: the beat or preparation on the lead hand or foot of the opponent, the disengagement, the simple thrust.

Any elementary offense or defense through proper strategy and ring generalship may, under the right conditions, be used in the most advanced type of fighting.

Any elementary offense or defense through proper strategy and ring generalship may be used in the most advanced type of fighting.

Training Aids

During lessons, the master will have made a point of explaining, *convincingly*, the tactical application of each stroke, whether of attack, defense or counterattack. In each case, he will have stressed:

HOW   — — —   it is done.

WHY   — — —   it is done.

WHEN   — — —   it is done.

If the lessons have included the variety of circumstances in which a stroke may have to be used, then again, the pupil is less likely to be surprised by an unfamiliar action.

Vary your partner and you will not be fixed at a specific tactic or cadence.

Once more, remember, a successful fighter is one who has learned to select, *correctly*, the strokes he has been taught.

One of the most important lessons is to master combinations (hands, feet, or both, etc.). Then, you must study the style of your opponent before deciding what combinations might beat him.

FIVE WAYS OF ATTACK

Editor's note: The five ways of attack were the last delineations Bruce was using to explain his movements just prior to his death. The incompleteness of his notes is most apparent here when compared to the extensive explanations he gave his personal students.

Study the style of your opponent before deciding what combinations might beat him.

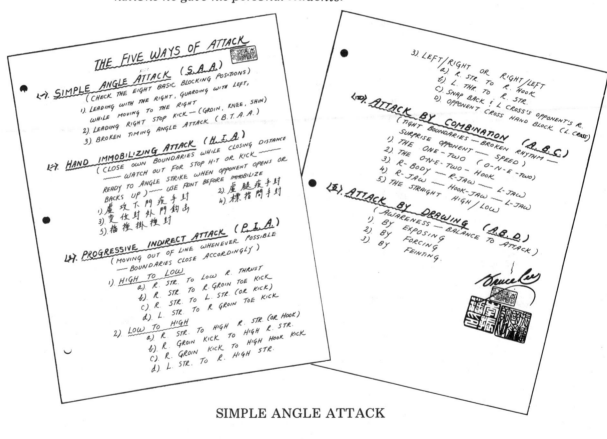

SIMPLE ANGLE ATTACK

SAA — The **simple angle attack** is any simple attack thrown at an unexpected angle, sometimes preceded by feinting. It is often set up by readjusting the distance with footwork. Study the *elusive lead* and *simple attack*.

IMMOBILIZATION ATTACK

IA — The **immobilization attack** is performed by applying an immobilizing preparation (trapping) on the opponent's head (hair), hand or leg as you crash the
line to engagement. The trapping keeps the opponent from moving that
part of his body, offering you a safety zone from which to strike. Immobilization attacks can be prepared (set-up) by using any of the other four ways
of attack and traps can be performed in combination or singularly. Study the
stop-hit as well.

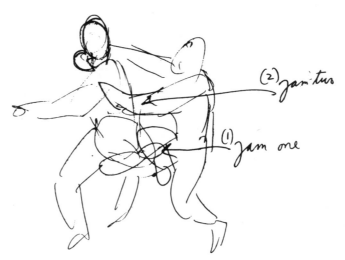

Remember, a
successful fighter
is one who has
learned to select,
correctly, the
strokes he has
been taught.

Immobilization may be used as a preventive measure when attacking with one hand by
pinning with the other. It may also be used as a preventive measure when slipping or
countering.

Using immobilization when an opponent actually intends to deliver a blow requires a
knowledge of when the opponent is going to lead and depends on speed and skill for
execution.

Get *body feel* on the forearm to use it as a
destructive weapon. Use a loose clawing snap
or club along with elbowing.

PROGRESSIVE INDIRECT ATTACK

PIA — The **progressive indirect attack** is preceded by a feint or an uncommitted
thrust designed to misdirect the opponent's actions or reactions in order to

hit the opening line or gain a period of movement-time. The progressive indirect attack is performed in a single forward motion without a withdrawal, as opposed to the single angulated attack preceded by a feint which is actually two movements. Study *feints* and *disengagements*.

The principal use of the progressive indirect attack is to overcome an opponent whose defense is strong and fast enough to deal with a simple direct attack. It is also used to offer variation in one's pattern of attack.

Remember, though PIA uses feints and disengagements, each progressive indirect attack is executed in a single, forward motion. It is *progressive* to gain distance. To shorten the distance, the measure has to be closed by a good *half* with your first feint. Prolong your feint enough to allow your opponent time to react. Leave to your second movement only the *second half* of the distance. Do not wait for the block before completing your attack; keep ahead of it.

Except in rare cases, all movements should be made as small as possible.

It is while the opponent's arm is traveling across, downward, upward, etc., that you must start your offensive action. That means, for a moment, his defense is moving in an opposite direction to your attack. Your attack, therefore, is made with a disengagement.

Except in rare cases, all movements should be made as small as possible, that is with the least deviation of the hand necessary to induce the opponent to react. Disengagements, likewise, should pass very close to the opponent's hand.

To make PIA with the leg more effective, try the one-and-a-half beat.

O-N-E: The first attack is deep, sudden, economical, well-covered and above all, well-balanced. Distinguish between one initiation for power (like the reverse hook) and a straight initiation.

AND-A-HALF: The second half must be a kick that is fast and powerful and that does not deviate too much from the on-guard position, as in-fighting may be initiated.

To reach the target, the attacker must deceive the adversary's forward moving balance, his rooted balance, his guards and parries and must catch him in a moment of physical or mental unpreparedness.

During combinations with feinting in the initial progression, *loosely* change to second

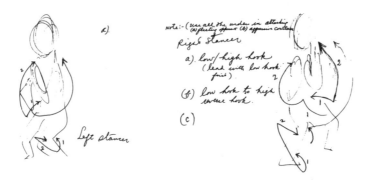

intention. Pay particular attention to the efficient gap-bridging of the two moves to get speed and power.

ATTACK BY COMBINATION

Combinations set the opponent up for a finishing knockout blow or kick.

ABC — The **attack by combination** is a series of thrusts that follow each other naturally and are generally thrown to more than one line. Study *compound attack* and *combination punching*.

Attacks by combination are generally composed of set-ups. The term "set-ups" denotes a series of blows and/or kicks delivered in a natural sequence. The object is to maneuver the opponent into such a position or create such an opening that the final blow of the series will find a vulnerable spot. Combinations set the opponent up for a finishing knockout blow or kick.

The difference between an expert and a novice fighter is that the expert makes use of each opportunity and follows up on each opening. He makes use of his sensitive and dominating aura and his imposing rhythm. He delivers his blows and/or kicks in a well-planned series, each opening creating another, until finally a clean shot is obtained.

———————————————————

Some blows seem to be "follow blows" in that they come after certain leads. For instance, the straight left is a follow blow for the right jab, and a right hook is a follow blow for the straight left.

———————————————————

It seems natural to punch straight and then hook and it seems natural to punch first to the head and then to the body.

The difference between an expert and a novice fighter is that the expert makes use of each opportunity.

Follow blows or set-ups have *rhythm* and *feel* as their basis. Punching in rhythm is an important factor in Western boxing.

———————————————————

Triple-blows are common in ABC. They may be thrown by first slipping to either the outside or inside and then delivering two body blows, followed by a blow to the head. The first two blows will bring down the adversary's guard, opening him up for the final thrust.

———————————————————

Another version of the triple blow set-up is known as the "safety triple." The safety triple is a series of blows which have rhythm as their basis in punching first to the body and then to the head or vice-versa. The main thing to remember is that the last blow will be to the spot of the first blow. If the first blow is to the jaw, the last blow will also be to the jaw.

———————————————————

Study also the one-two variations.

Be exposed to the various paths of combinations and be able to change the path *during* execution.

Be expose to the varion paths of combination and to change path during one path.

ATTACK BY DRAWING

ABD — The **attack by drawing** is an attack or counterattack initiated upon luring the opponent into a commitment by leaving him an apparent opening or executing movements that he may try to time and counter. Attack by drawing may make use of the previous four ways of attack. Study *timing* and the *eight basic defense positions*.

It's usually best, whenever possible, to draw your opponent into leading before hitting out on your own account. By forcing your opponent to *commit* himself to a decided step, you can be moderately certain of what he is about to do. His commitment will deprive him of the ability to change his position and guard swiftly enough to deal successfully with any offensive you may yourself adopt.

By his mere action of hitting out, you will or should secure an opening of sorts. You should make him present you with a fair target at which to aim.

Most important of all, you will have borrowed some very considerable force from him to add to the power of your own counter. Remember, the whole secret of hard hitting lies in accurate timing, correct placement *and* mental application.

Keep your awareness and balance to attack after drawing his commitment by exposing a target to him, by forcing (closing with or without immobilization, slow or fast) and by feinting an attack that he will try to counter.

Remember, the whole secret of hard hitting lies in accurate timing, correct placement and mental application.

CIRCLE WITH NO CIRCUMFERENCE

Jeet Kune Do, ultimately, is not a matter of petty technique but of highly developed personal spirituality and physique. It is not a question of developing what has already been developed but of recovering what has been left behind. These things have been with us, in us, all the time and have never been lost or distorted except by our misguided manipulation of them. Jeet Kune Do is not a matter of technology but of spiritual insight and training.

The tools are at an undifferentiated center of a circle that has no circumference, moving and yet not moving, in tension and yet relaxed, seeing everything happening and yet not at all anxious about its outcome, with nothing purposely designed, nothing consciously calculated, no anticipation, no expectation — in short, standing innocently like a baby and yet, with all the cunning, subterfuge and keen intelligence of a fully mature mind.

Leave sagehood behind and enter once more into ordinary humanity. After coming to understand the other side, come back and live on this side. After the cultivation of no-cultivation, one's thoughts continue to be detached from phenomenal things and one still remains amid the phenomenal, yet devoid of the phenomenal.

To float in totality, to have no technique, is to have all technique.

Both the man and his surroundings are eliminated. Then, neither the man nor his surroundings are eliminated. Walk on!

One can never be the master of his technical knowledge unless all his psychic hindrances are removed and he can keep his mind in a state of emptiness (fluidity), even purged of whatever technique he has obtained.

With all the training thrown to the wind, with a mind perfectly unaware of its own working, with the self vanishing nowhere, anybody knows where, the art of Jeet Kune Do attains its perfection.

The more aware you become, the more you shed from day to day what you have learned so that your mind is always fresh and uncontaminated by previous conditioning.

Learning techniques corresponds to an intellectual apprehension of the philosophies in Zen, and in both Zen and Jeet Kune Do, an intellectual proficiency does not cover the whole ground of the discipline. Both require the attainment of ultimate reality, which is the emptiness or the absolute. The latter transcends all modes of relativity.

In Jeet Kune Do, all technique is to be forgotten and the unconscious is to be left alone to handle the situation. The technique will assert its wonders automatically or spontaneously. To float in totality, to have no technique, is to have all technique.

The knowledge and skill you have achieved are meant to be "forgotten" so you can float comfortably in emptiness, without obstruction. Learning is important but do not become its slave. Above all, do not harbor anything external and superfluous — the mind is primary. Any technique, however worthy and desirable, becomes a disease when the mind is obsessed with it.

The six diseases:

1. The desire for victory.
2. The desire to resort to technical cunning.
3. The desire to display all that has been learned.
4. The desire to awe the enemy.
5. The desire to play the passive role.
6. The desire to get rid of whatever disease one is affected by.

> The spirit is no doubt the controlling agent of our existence.

"To desire" is an attachment. "To desire not to desire" is also an attachment. To be unattached then, means to be free at once from both statements, positive and negative. This is to be simultaneously both "yes" and "no," which is intellectually absurd. However, not so in Zen.

Nirvana is to be consciously unconscious or to be unconsciously conscious. That is its secret. The act is so direct and immediate that intellectualization finds no room to insert itself and cut the act to pieces.

The spirit is no doubt the controlling agent of our existence. This invisible seat controls every movement in whatever external situation arises. It is thus, to be extremely mobile, never "stopping" in any place at any moment. Preserve this state of spiritual freedom and non-attachment as soon as you assume the fighting stance. Be "master of the house."

It is the ego that stands rigidly against influences from the outside, and it is this "ego rigidity" that makes it impossible for us to accept everything that confronts us.

201

Art lives where absolute freedom is, because where it is not, there can be no creativity.

Seek not the cultivated innocence of a clever mind that wants to be innocent, but have rather that state of innocence where there is no denial or acceptance and the mind just sees what *is*.

All goals apart from the means are illusions. Becoming is a denial of being.

By an error repeated throughout the ages, truth, becoming a law or a faith, places obstacles in the way of knowledge. Method, which is in its very substance ignorance, encloses truth within a vicious circle. We should break such a circle, not by seeking knowledge, but by discovering the cause of ignorance.

Recollection and anticipation are fine qualities of consciousness that distinguish the human mind from that of the lower animals. But, when actions are directly related to the problem of life and death, these properties must be relinquished for the sake of fluidity of thought and lightning rapidity of action.

Action is our relationship to everything.

Action is our relationship to everything. Action is not a matter of right and wrong. It is only when action is partial that there is a right and a wrong.

Don't let your attention be arrested! Transcend dualistic comprehension of a situation.

Give up thinking as though not giving it up. Observe the techniques as though not observing. Utilize the art as a means to advance in the study of the Way.

Prajna immovable doesn't mean immovability or insensibility. It means that the mind is endowed with capabilities of infinite, instantaneous motion that knows no hindrance.

Make the tools see. All movements come out of emptiness and the mind is the name given to this dynamic aspect of emptiness. It is straight, without ego-centered motivation. The emptiness is sincerity, genuineness and straightforwardness, allowing nothing between itself and its movements.

Jeet Kune Do exists in your not seeing me and my not seeing you, where yin and yang have not yet differentiated themselves.

Jeet Kune Do dislikes partialization or localization. Totality can meet all situations.

―――――――――――

When the mind is fluid, the moon is in the stream where it is at once movable and immovable. The waters are in motion all the time, but the moon retains its serenity. The mind moves in response to ten thousand situations but remains ever the same.

―――――――――――

The stillness in stillness is not the real stillness; only when there is stillness in movement does the universal rhythm manifest itself. To change with change is the changeless state. Nothingness cannot be confined; the softest thing cannot be snapped.

―――――――――――

Assume the *pristine purity.* In order to display your native activities to the utmost limit, remove all psychic obstruction.

―――――――――――

Would that we could at once strike with the eyes! In the long way from the eye through the arm to the fist, how much is lost!

―――――――――――

Sharpen the psychic power of seeing in order to act immediately in accordance with what you see. Seeing takes place with the inner mind.

In the long way from the eye through the arm to the fist, how much is lost!

―――――――――――

Because one's self-consciousness or ego-consciousness is too conspicuously present over the entire range of his attention, it interferes with his free display of whatever proficiency he has so far acquired or is going to acquire. One should remove this obtruding self or ego-consciousness and apply himself to the work to be done as if nothing particular were taking place at the moment.

―――――――――――

To be of no-mind means to assume the everyday mind.

―――――――――――

The mind must be wide open to function freely in thought. A limited mind cannot think freely.

―――――――――――

A concentrated mind is not an attentive mind, but a mind that is in the state of awareness can concentrate. Awareness is never exclusive; it includes everything.

―――――――――――

Not being tense but ready, not thinking yet not dreaming, not being set but flexible — it is being wholly and quietly alive, aware and alert, ready for whatever may come.

The Jeet Kune Do man should be on the alert to meet the interchangeability of opposites. As soon as his mind "stops" with either of them, it loses its own fluidity. A JKD man should keep his mind always in the state of emptiness so that his freedom in action will never be obstructed.

The *abiding stage* is the point where the mind hesitates to abide. It attaches itself to an object and stops the flow.

The deluded mind is the mind affectively burdened by intellect. Thus, it cannot move without stopping and reflecting on itself. This obstructs its native fluidity.

The wheel revolves when it is not too tightly attached to the axle. When the mind is tied up, it feels inhibited in every move it makes and nothing is accomplished with spontaneity. Its work will be of poor quality or it may never be finished at all.

When there is no center and no circumference, then there is truth.

When the mind is tethered to a center, naturally it is not free. It can move only within the limits of that center. If one is isolated, he is dead; he is paralyzed within the fortress of his own ideas.

When you are completely aware, there is no space for a conception, a scheme, "the opponent and I;" there is complete abandonment.

When there is no obstruction, the JKD man's movements are like flashes of lightning or like the mirror reflecting images.

When insubstantiality and substantiality are not set and defined, when there is no track to change what is, one has mastered the formless form. When there is clinging to form, when there is attachment of the mind, it is not the true path. When technique comes out of itself, that is the way.

Jeet Kune Do is the art not founded on techniques or doctrine. It is *just as you are.*

When there is no center and no circumference, then there is truth. When you freely express, you are the total style.

IT'S JUST A NAME

There is a powerful craving in most of us to see ourselves as instruments in the hands of others and, thus, free ourselves from responsibility for acts which are prompted by our own questionable inclinations and impulses. Both the strong and the weak grasp at this alibi. The latter hide their malevolence under the virtue of obedience. The strong, too, claim absolution by proclaiming themselves the chosen instruments of a higher power — God, history, fate, nation or humanity.

———————————

Similarly, we have more faith in what we imitate than in what we originate. We cannot derive a sense of absolute certitude from anything which has its roots in us. The most poignant sense of insecurity comes from standing alone and we are not alone when we imitate. It is thus with most of us; we are what other people say we are. We know ourselves chiefly by hearsay.

———————————

To become different from what we are, we must have some awareness of what we are. Whether this being different results in dissimulation or a real change of heart, it cannot be realized without self-awareness. Yet, it is remarkable that the very people who are most self-dissatisfied, who crave most for a new identity, have the least self-awareness. They have turned away from an unwanted self and, hence, never had a good look at it. The result is that most dissatisfied people can neither dissimulate nor attain a real change of heart. They are transparent and their unwanted qualities persist through all attempts at self-dramatization and self-transformation. It is the lack of self-awareness which renders us transparent. The soul that knows itself is opaque.

> The soul that knows itself is opaque.

———————————

Fear comes from uncertainty. When we are absolutely certain, whether of our worth or our worthlessness, we are almost impervious to fear. Thus, a feeling of utter unworthiness can be a source of courage. Everything seems possible when we are absolutely helpless or absolutely powerful — and both states stimulate our gullibility.

———————————

Pride is a sense of worth derived from something that is not organically part of us, while self-esteem is derived from the potentialities and achievements of self. We are proud when we identify ourselves with an imaginary self, a leader, a holy cause, a collective body or possessions. There is fear and intolerance in pride; it is sensitive and uncompromising. The less promise and potentiality in the self, the more imperative is the need for pride. The core of pride is self-rejection. It is true, however, that when pride releases energies and serves as a spur to achievement, it can lead to a reconciliation with the self and the attainment of genuine self-esteem.

———————————

Secretiveness can be a source of pride. It is a paradox that secretiveness plays the same role as boasting — both are engaged in the creation of a disguise. Boasting tries to create

an imaginary self, while secretiveness gives us the exhilarating feeling of being princes disguised in meekness. Of the two, secretiveness is the more difficult and effective. For the self-observant, boasting breeds self-contempt. Yet, it is as Spinoza said: "Men govern nothing with more difficulty than their tongues, and they can moderate their desires more than their words." Humility, however, is not verbal renunciation of pride but the substitution of pride for self-awareness and objectivity. Forced humility is false pride.

A fateful process is set in motion when the individual is released "to the freedom of his own impotence" and left to justify his existence by his own efforts. The individual on his own, striving to realize himself and prove his worth, has created all that is great in literature, art, music, science and technology. This autonomous individual, also, when he can neither realize himself nor justify his existence by his own efforts, is a breeding ground of frustration and the seed of the convulsion that shakes our world to its foundations.

Action is a high road to self-confidence and esteem.

The autonomous individual is stable only so long as he is possessed of self-esteem. The maintenance of self-esteem is a continuous task which taxes all of the individual's power and inner resources. We have to prove our worth and justify our existence anew each day. When, for whatever reason, self-esteem is unattainable, the autonomous individual becomes a highly explosive entity. He turns away from an unpromising self and plunges into the pursuit of pride, the explosive substitute for self-esteem. All social disturbances and upheavals have their roots in crises of individual self-esteem, and the great endeavor in which the masses most readily unite is basically a search for pride.

So, we acquire a sense of worth either by realizing our talents, or by keeping busy or by identifying ourselves with something apart from us — be it a cause, a leader, a group, possessions or whatnot. The path of self-realization is the most difficult. It is taken only when other avenues to a sense of worth are more or less blocked. Men of talent have to be encouraged and goaded to engage in creative work. Their groans and laments echo through the ages.

Action is a high road to self-confidence and esteem. Where it is open, all energies flow toward it. It comes readily to most people and its rewards are tangible. The cultivation of the spirit is elusive and difficult and the tendency toward it is rarely spontaneous, whereas, the opportunities for action are many.

The propensity to action is symptomatic of an inner unbalance. To be balanced is to be more or less at rest. Action is at the bottom — a swinging and flailing of the arms to regain one's balance and keep afloat. And if it is true, as Napolean wrote to Carnot,

"The art of government is not to let men grow stale," then, it is an art of unbalancing. The crucial difference between a totalitarian regime and a free social order is, perhaps, in the methods of unbalancing by which their people are kept active and striving.

We are told that talent creates its own opportunities. Yet, it sometimes seems that intense desire creates not only its own opportunities, but its own talents as well.

The times of drastic change are times of passions. We can never be fit and ready for that which is wholly new. We have to adjust ourselves and every radical adjustment is a crisis in self-esteem: we undergo a test; we have to prove ourselves. A population subjected to drastic change is, thus, a population of misfits, and misfits live and breathe in an atmosphere of passion.

That we pursue something passionately does not always mean that we really want it or have a special aptitude for it. Often, the thing we pursue most passionately is but a substitute for the one thing we really want and cannot have. It is usually safe to predict that the fulfillment of an excessively cherished desire is not likely to still our nagging anxiety. In every passionate pursuit, the pursuit counts more than the object pursued.

In every passionate pursuit, the pursuit counts more than the object pursued.

Our sense of power is more vivid when we break a man's spirit than when we win his heart, for we can win a man's heart one day and lose it the next. But when we break a proud spirit, we achieve something that is final and absolute.

It is compassion rather than the principle of justice which can guard us against being unjust to our fellow men.

It is doubtful whether there is such a thing as impulsive or natural tolerance. Tolerance requires an effort of thought and self-control. Acts of kindness, too, are rarely without deliberation and "thoughtfulness." Thus, it seems that some artificiality, some posing and pretense, is inseparable from any act or attitude which involves a limitation of our appetites and selfishness. We ought to beware of people who do not think it necessary to pretend that they are good and decent. Lack of hypocrisy in such things hints at a capacity for a more depraved ruthlessness. Pretense is often an indispensable step in the attainment of genuineness. It is a form into which genuine inclinations flow and solidify.

The control of our being is not unlike the combination of a safe. One turn of the knob rarely unlocks the safe; each advance and retreat is a step toward one's final achievement.

Jeet Kune Do is not to hurt, but is one of the avenues through which life opens its secrets to us. We can see through others only when we can see through ourselves and Jeet Kune Do is a step toward knowing oneself.

Self-knowledge is the basis of Jeet Kune Do because it is effective, not only for the individual's martial art, but also for his life as a human being.

Learning Jeet Kune Do is not a matter seeking knowledge or accumulating stylized pattern, but is discovering the cause of ignorance.

If people say Jeet Kune Do is different from "this" or from "that," then let the name of Jeet Kune Do be wiped out, for that is what it is, just a name. Please don't fuss over it.

ACKNOWLEDGEMENT

I'd like to express my sincere appreciation to Gil Johnson who has done an excellent job of organizing a mountain of material; to Geri Simon for her graphic design; to Dan Inosanto, Bruce's assistant and close friend, and other JKD students who are dedicated to preserving and expanding Bruce's ideas; and to Ohara Publications, especially M. Uyehara and Dick Hennessy, who out of long friendship and respect for Bruce, have faithfully reproduced his original notes and drawings.

Linda Lee